The Way to Write for Children

Joan Aiken's previous books include:

For adults: The Young Lady from Paris
The Weeping Ash
The Smile of the Stranger
The Five-Minute Marriage
Voices in an Empty House

For children: The Stolen Lake
The Shadow Guests
A Touch of Chill
Go Saddle the Sea
Arabel's Raven
Midnight is a Place
The Wolves of Willoughby Chase

Plays: Moon Mill
Street
The Mooncusser's Daughter
Winterthing

The Way to Write for Children

JOAN AIKEN

St. Martin's Press
New York

Library of Congress Cataloging in Publication Data

Aiken, Joan, 1924—
   The way to write for children.

   1. Children's literature—Technique.   I. Title.
PN147.5.A37   1983   808.06'8   82-10692
ISBN 0-312-85839-6

First published in Great Britain by Elm Tree Books Ltd.

First U.S. Edition
10 9 8 7 6 5 4 3 2 1

Contents

Acknowledgements

The author and publishers would like to thank the following for permission to use copyright material:

Edward Arnold (Publishers) Ltd for *Aspects of the Novel* by E. M. Forster;

Chatto & Windus Ltd and Russell & Volkening Inc. for *Earthly Powers* © 1977 by Anne Tyler;

Coward, McCann & Geoghegan Inc. for *Millions of Cats* © 1929 by Wanda Gag;

Curtis Brown Ltd, London, for *The Only Child* by James Kirkup;

Evans Brothers Ltd for *Children and Fiction* by E. W. Hildick;

Eyre Methuen Ltd and E. P. Dutton Inc. for *Six Characters in Search of an Author* from *Naked Masks: Five Plays by Luigi Pirandello* edited by Eric Bentley, © 1952 by E. P. Dutton & Co. Inc, renewed © 1980 by Eric Bentley;

Samuel French Ltd for *The Burnt Flower Bed* by Ugo Betti and *The Physicists* by Friedrich Durrenmatt;

Elaine Greene Ltd for *Blue Skies, Brown Studies* by William Sansom;

Elaine Greene Ltd and International Creative Management for *There Must Be A Pony* © 1960 by James Kirkwood;

Hamish Hamilton Ltd and Mrs Helen Thurber for *My Life and Hard Times* and *Fables for our Time* by James Thurber;

A. M. Heath & Co. Ltd for *Life with Lisa* by Sybil Burr, published by Penguin Books Ltd;

David Higham Associates Ltd for *The Witch in the Wood* by T. H. White, published by William Collins, Son & Co. Ltd;

The Hogarth Press for *Cider With Rosie* by Laurie Lee;

Oxford University Press for *Lark Rise to Candleford* by Flora Thompson and *Three Houses* by Angela Thirkel;

A. D. Peters & Co. Ltd for *Cautionary Tales* by Hilaire Belloc, published by Gerald Duckworth & Co. Ltd;

Laurence Pollinger Ltd for *The Lost Childhood* from *Collected Essays* by Graham Greene, published by the Bodley Head;

G. P. Putnam's Sons for *The Anatomy of Humour* from *Spilt Milk,* © 1942, renewed © 1969 by Morris Bishop;

Random House Inc. for *My Side of the Matter* from *Selected Writings of Truman Capote*;

The Society of Authors, as the literary representative of the Estate of A. E. Housman, and Jonathan Cape Ltd for Poem XXXVII (*I Did Not Lose My Heart*) from *Collected Poems* by A. E. Housman;

Thames & Hudson Ltd for *The Uses of Enchantment* by Bruno Bettelheim;

Ward Lock Educational Co. Ltd for *Fiction for Children and Adults* by Myles McDowell and *How Children Respond to Fiction* by Nicholas Tucker from *Children's Literature in Education;*

A. P. Watt Ltd for *Just So Stories, Red Dog* from *The Two Jungle Books* and letters of Rudyard Kipling, published by Macmillan Publishers Ltd, and for *The Glums* by Frank Muir and Denis Norden.

The Way to Write for Children

Chapter One

Do you want to write *about* children or *for* them?

The title of this work is misleading — a hazard contingent upon providing a contribution to an existent series — because, of course, there is no *one* way in which to write for children.

Ways of writing for children vary as widely as ways of writing for adults; and may be as numerous as the writers who find and follow them.

But there are, perhaps, better and worse ways; and there may be ways in which *not* to write for children; all of which it will be the task of the present work to discuss.

An author, or prospective author, who has the intention of writing for children may do well to ask himself, first, a few questions of a basic nature.

The first: is this to be a book *for* children, or a book *about* children? The two things are not necessarily synonymous. The painter Balthus painted beautiful pictures of little girls; but they were not intended for little girls to look at. Are you, when you write, eager to explore the mind and feelings of a child, analyse his relationship to the world about him, recall the joys and terrors of your own childhood?

Or do you merely want to tell a story that you think children will enjoy?

A brief glance at history may here be illustrative.

During the nineteenth century, the production and publishing of books intended for children became a thriving industry in the English-speaking world. It gathered momentum from *The Butterfly Ball* in 1807, George Cruikshank's *Fairy Library* and translations of the Grimm brothers' tales in the 1820s, through *Jessica's First Prayer* by Sarah Smith in 1866 (which sold one and a half million copies), Charlotte M. Yonge's novels for young people, Ruskin, Thackeray, Mrs Molesworth, Mrs Ewing, Lewis Carroll (to mention only a few landmarks) and, towards the latter part of the century, Louisa M. Alcott, Mark Twain, Laurence Housman, Edith Nesbit and Rudyard Kipling.

During about eighty years, children's literature had become an established professional form. Some of the writers created new and original material of a highly imaginative order, some revived or rewrote existing folk tales or legends, some produced moral and instructive tracts, modelled on Thomas Day's eighteenth-century *Sandford and Merton,* which contrasted the fortunes of good and bad children. *Struwwelpeter* and the Taylor sisters' *Meddlesome Matty* are later examples of this genre.

Then, during the last quarter of the nineteenth century a new phenomenon appeared: stories ostensibly intended for children, but really meant for the diversion of adults. *Helen's Babies* by the American John Habberton, in 1876, a farcical story about a bachelor uncle left in charge of two small nephews, Budge and Toddy, was one of the innovators in this field; it had a huge success and seeded a whole crop of imitators.

A work of genius, Mark Twain's *Huckleberry Finn,* which appeared in 1884, presented an adult story, and a view of the inconsistencies and injustices of the adult world, as observed with the primitive shrewdness of an untaught boy.

These two books were forerunners, and started a fashion for childhood in adult literature. Kenneth Grahame wrote *Dream Days* and *The Golden Age,* anecdotes from nursery life, purporting to be addressed to the young, but couched in elaborate stylish whimsical language. These stories appeared originally in Scribners Magazine, evidence enough that they were really meant for adults. *The Wind in the Willows,* Grahame's most famous work, suffers from internal imbalance; parts of the narrative, those about Rat, Mole, and Toad, are simple, lively and affectionately told, plainly with real children in mind; but the mystical sections and the descriptive passages are often highflown and pretentious, written with an eye on adult readership. An American, Bertram Smith, followed with *Days of Discovery* in 1917, closely modelled on *Dream Days,* and suffering from the same kind of facetiousness.

In 1897 appeared Henry James's *What Maisie Knew,* a story of adult philandering seen through a child's eyes. Two years later Kipling produced *Stalky & Co,* memories of schooldays at the United Services College, seen through the eyes of adult experience. *Stalky* has now come to be accepted as a juvenile book, but internal evidence, the fact that the stories first appeared in The Windsor Magazine, and the wholly adult style and references (quite different from the same author's *Puck of Pook's Hill* or *The Jungle Books*) suggests that Kipling was indulging in reminiscences of a rather wish-fulfilling kind, for the benefit of his own contemporaries.

In short, the child's-eye viewpoint had caught on in the adult market; and it has remained in fashion ever since, though many such books tend to overlap from one readership into the other. Salinger's *The Catcher in the Rye,* McCullers's *The Member of the Wedding,* Jim Kirkwood's *There Must Be a Pony,* are later examples.

From this short survey we learn that, in a work of fiction, the fact that the main protagonist or narrator is a child may be no guarantee that the work is actually intended to be read *by* children. Several nineteenth century books (for example *Jane Eyre* and *David Copperfield*) have fallen victim to the notion that a story told by a child must be suitable juvenile reading: a misunderstanding that leads to boredom, mystification, and unfair dislike of the works so misused.

Therefore: before you begin to write, make sure that you are clear in your own mind whether you are writing *about* children, or *for* them. Have you a reader — or readers — in prospect? (Readers are kittle cattle, of course, and the final outcome may not be what you expect by any means; plenty of books written for children find their way into the adult market, and vice versa); but unless you, the writer, have a definite X-reader, possibly yourself, established as the target towards whom you are aiming your story, the work will be likely to waver and vacillate, to fall between two styles, or two stools.

For the benefit and clarification of your style and purpose, accordingly, establish to your own satisfaction, before you start, whether you intend to write *Lolita* or *Goldilocks; Lord of the Flies* or *Little Lord Fauntleroy; Jonathan Livingston Seagull* or *Jemima Puddleduck; Rebecca* or *Rebecca of Sunnybrook Farm; Claudine at School* or *What Katy Did.*

If there is any doubt or ambiguity about this, your work will suffer. If you try to write for children, but hope that adults will be reading the book too, an element of archness or insincerity is almost certain to creep into your style. And if your book overlaps the two different areas, your publishers may not be sure who is going to buy it, and so promotion and sales will suffer.

Adults and children read in different ways

> The strongest and most influential memories are almost always those of childhood.
>
> Fyodor Dostoevsky

Once he is at work, of course, a writer should not be thinking about his readers; but in order to analyse the difference between writing for children, and for adults, it is useful to stop and think, beforehand: who might read this book? In what way will they read it?

Adults and children read in very different ways, and for very different reasons.

> A good children's book makes complex experience available to its readers; a good adult book draws attention to the inescapable complexity of an experience.
> Myles McDowell, *Fiction for Children and Adults: Children's Literature in Education*

Here are what I feel to be some of the main differences between adult and children's reading.

Adult reading falls roughly into two categories: serious and light. 'Oh, I don't read *that* sort of book except when I am on holiday,' many people say — *that* sort of book denoting anything that demands sustained mental effort. A fairly large percentage of adult readers, for their routine reading-matter, want something that won't overtax their minds, fatigued by the day's toil: probably a whodunnit, a spy-story, or a piece of light romance.

The requirements of children, on the other hand, are absolutely different; children have plenty of energy, they aren't exhausted by the day's toil, and it is to be hoped they don't have serious problems from which their minds need diverting. Nor are their minds scribbled over already with preconceived notions, prejudices, and accumulations of acquired impressions. Children read to *learn* — even when they are reading fantasy, nonsense, light verse, comics, or the copy on cereal packets, they are expanding their minds all the time, enlarging their vocabulary, making discoveries; it is all new to them.

> Maxima debetur puero reverentia. (The greatest respect is due to young persons.)
> Juvenal, *Satires xiii*

So the writer's responsibility to his reader is wholly different in each of these two cases. For the adult he has merely to amuse, entertain, and distract; towards the child, his responsibility is much — I won't say heavier, because that sounds ponderous and gloomy — but just, more of a responsibility.

An adult reader will, inevitably, have read dozens, perhaps hundreds of similar books before he picks up yours; but a child reader may, literally, be encountering your book as his first real reading experience. One has to bear this in mind as a possibility. I have occasionally had people say to me: 'My son — or daughter — read your book such-and-such. It was the first book he read right through by himself.' This is a solemn thought. The first book that a child reads has a colossal impact.

Think back to your own first reading experience, whatever it was — and you will see what I mean.

> I do not know how I learned to read. I only remember my first books and their effect upon me; it is from my earliest reading that I date the unbroken consciousness of my own existence.
>
> Jean-Jacques Rousseau, *Confessions*

Naturally one does not sit pen — or typewriter — in hand, thinking, 'These may be the first words that somebody reads' — but, just the same, the consciousness is, or should be, there, tucked away at the back, encouraging you to think hard and maintain a high standard.

With adult readers, the situation is just the reverse. If you write thrillers, for instance, you may be sure that your readers will be thriller aficionados. Thriller readers read more and more thrillers. Romance readers read all the romances they can find. Therefore the writer knows that his reader has a common vocabulary of experience — a common code of situations, characters, fictional clichés, as it were: a fund, a bank which is shared between writer and reader. So when writing thrillers or romances for adults, it is permissible to use code characters, the Mr Rochester-type hero, the Gothic castle, the locked room, and readers will accept this usage, and, indeed, go half-way to meet you. 'She was an acidulated spinster.' 'He was a ruthless, selfmade businessman.' 'Their son was a long-haired, guitar-playing hippie.' 'Uncle Jack was a remittance-man, a black sheep in Australia.' The seedy spy, the absent-

5

minded professor, the dreamy poet, the haughty aristocratic old lady — these are all legitimate stock-in-trade characters for the romance or thriller writer, who uses a whole series of shortcuts, and economises on character so as to get in plenty of action.

Childhood enjoys a limited privilege of strength . . . the knowledge being narrow, the interest is narrow in the objects of knowledge: consequently the sensibilities are not scattered . . .

De Quincey

But in a children's book *no* such usages are permissible; the characters must be real, rounded-out individuals. Over-elaborate description is not required; I don't know that Mark Twain ever gives any indication of what Tom Sawyer and Huck Finn looked like; that isn't needed. We know those boys, we know that Tom is rather sententious and given to making rules, that Huck is devoured by moral problems; we know how they would act at any time; we don't have to be told what their external appearance was like.

When it comes to place or setting, some description is essential for children. They shouldn't be swamped, or their interest will slacken; but, on the assumption that, if your book is set in a New York subway station, a Welsh valley, an Indian jungle, or a London suburb, ninety per cent of your readers will not have the least conception of what the place looks like, it is your duty by them to produce a rapid, vivid picture, with enough details to nail it in their minds.

They passed the region where fields of cabbages and rows of yellow brick cottages mark the division between London and the suburbs . . . then the lamp posts in the road got fewer, and the fields got greener and the hedges thicker — it was real, true country.

E. Nesbit, *Nine Unlikely Tales.*

Adult readers have acquired bad habits in the course of their lives.

'What (said Elphinstone) have you read it through?' 'No, Sir, do *you* read books *through?*'

Boswell's *Life of Johnson*

They have a tendency to skip. The writer may be wasting his time putting in carefully worded description for them. It is justifiable, and very economical, to say, 'She lived in a garret in Paris.' The adult reader *knows* what a garret in Paris is like — if he hasn't been in one, he has seen it on the movies, or read Balzac or Hugo. But your child reader has no preconceived notions about the garret in Paris, and towards him you have a duty to depict it clearly but as economically as possible.

I have said that adult readers have a tendency to skip.

But in this connection we come to a curious anomaly. There are things in fiction known as bridge passages. Every writer knows what a pain they can be to construct. You have to have them — yet to a large proportion of writers they don't come naturally. Flaubert fell into despair, trying to get his wretched heroine to walk into an inn and talk to a minor character.

A lot of adult readers are tremendous sticklers for bridge passages. 'Oh, I don't read it for the plot,' they say loftily, 'but for the incidental information about bell-ringing — or the Adriatic coast — or the Luddites — or the flora of North China.' I can remember my best friend at school saying that to me about *Gone With the Wind:* 'I didn't read it for the story, what I liked were the details about the American Civil War.' And I, cynical little beast, didn't believe her. I knew full well that, like the rest of us, she read it to see whether Rhett and Scarlett would be reunited at the end. But listening to my friend I realised — unconsciously then, consciously now — that she had already grown a stage beyond me, she was beginning to acquire the Calvinism and hypocrisy of adults.

For here comes my anomaly. Adults often skip the bridge passages and long descriptive bits; they justify this by saying they knew all that before anyway. But just the same they feel bridge passages are necessary, because they have a puritan yearning to be done good to.

So it is an unwritten rule that bridge passages must be provided for the grown-ups, which they are at liberty to skip if so minded.

With children the boot is on the other foot.

What do we get to equal the excitement and revelation in those first fourteen years?

Graham Greene,
The Lost Childhood and Other Essays

Children may be fiends in all kinds of ways, but they are not hypocrites. If you remember, it was a child who cut through all the pretence and pointed out that the Emperor had no clothes on. Children don't pretend to like things that bore them. For a start, they are not interested in bridge passages. Indeed, bridge passages are things that *in no circumstances whatever* should be allowed to find their way into a children's book. Here, the action should be continuous; and if there is a need to impart information, it must be imparted in the form of dialogue, or in little, chewable nuggets, sandwiched among the action.

Bridge passages are absolutely out.

So are flashbacks. Jane Austen, who, we may assume, had no admiration for flashbacks, since she never employed them, remarks in *Northanger Abbey:* 'This brief account of the family is intended to supersede the necessity of a long and minute detail from Mrs Thorpe herself, of her past adventures and sufferings, which might otherwise be expected to occupy the three or four following chapters, in which the worthlessness of lords and attornies might be set forth; and conversations which had passed away twenty years before be minutely repeated.'

No flashbacks. If you have to give information about something that took place in the past, find some other way in which to convey it — and not in a long piece of reminiscence by one of the characters. Better, perhaps, go back and begin your book at the earlier point?

Lengthy soliloquies are also taboo; so are inner ruminations, unless kept short, preferably to not more than two or three sentences; so are abrupt changes in time sequence, back-to-front chronological order, leaps about in time, or other such variations as adult readers are prepared to countenance. (Of course these rules are arbitrary, and have been broken: by Alan Garner, for example, in *Red Shift,* by Penelope Farmer in *Charlotte Sometimes,* by E. Nesbit in *Harding's Luck;* rules are made to be broken; but as a beginner children's writer you don't want to load the scales against yourself by piling on difficulties.)

A lady at the B.B.C. also told me that children can't adjust to switches in the narrative from one set of characters to another; but this I have not found to be true. Indeed I personally use that technique quite a lot, leaving one set of characters in some awkward predicament while transferring to others, in order to heighten tension. And I have not noticed that the books in which I have done this sell any less well than those with a single continuous narrative line.

Another thing that children strongly dislike is confidential asides from writer to reader, a form of self-indulgence that Trollope, for instance, committed a great deal: 'Mr Gilmore is to be our hero — or, at least, one of the two. The author will not, in these early words, declare that the squire will be his *favourite* hero, as he will wish that his readers should form their own opinions on the matter.' (*The Vicar of Bullhampton*)

A child reader would probably shut the book at that point. Children can't stand such coyness, and it is impossible to blame them, for it instantly lowers credulity to freezing-point. Trollope is such a great writer that we have to forgive him; he is playing a kind of game with the reader, all that we are doing is just for fun, not to be taken seriously, we have agreed to suspend our disbelief. But children are not reading for fun; for them it is all deadly serious.

E. Nesbit was occasionally guilty of an aside to the reader; it is her only fault.

Now we come up against another fundamental difference between the reading habits of adults and of children. A grown-up, however exhausted at the end of his hardworking day, however trivial the piece of reading matter in hand, can hardly help reading with a certain critical awareness. He has read this kind of thing before; he has standards of comparison; he is conscious of what the writer is trying to do to him.

Whereas the child reads quite *un*critically; he has never encountered anything of this kind before; or, we cannot assume that he has.

> I read every book that came in my way without distinction.
> Samuel Taylor Coleridge, *Letter to Poole,* 1797

An adult, watching a film, will recognise a movie actor and know this is to be the hero; the child may draw conclusions from the actor's face and general demeanour, but he won't have any certainty about it. And such experience as he has to draw on will be limited, highly significant on this account, and therefore possibly misleading. If a picture of a princess in a fairy tale reminds your reader of a kindergarten teacher who used to shout at the class when she was angry, it may set up a series of responses wholly unplanned and quite contradictory to those intended by the writer.

Children, furthermore, often actively hate criticism of their favourite reading-matter. For them the books they love are gospel;

criticism is sacrilege, because it breaks the bubble of credulity. An adult may read with critical reservations about the book's style, or construction, or character; this, for him, is part of the enjoyment. But it might not occur to a child that a book *could* be written in any other way; for him such analysis might actually destroy or murder a work.

Because children don't criticise, don't enjoy criticism, and read wholly for the plot, it is therefore the writer's duty to keep the narrative in a children's story as smooth as possible, not to interrupt it with asides to the reader, authorial comments, or any other hindrances.

Obviously, as children grow and read more, their tastes will become more sophisticated. But I think a writer has an obligation to assume that his work may be read by an archetypal beginner reader, and should set its measure accordingly.

> Literature breeds distress.
> Hilaire Belloc, *Cautionary Tales*

Adult readers can be masochistic.

Adults, during the process of growing up, have learned to overcome their repugnance and to eat oysters, snails, tripe, to drink tequila, ouzo, koumiss; with the same perversity some, in their reading, may be prepared to struggle with almost unintelligible obscurity, ponderous length, hair-raising obscenity, bloodcurdling violence, harrowing despair, or sheer stunning boredom.

But children won't eat oysters or snails. And though they will, of course, gobble junk foods if they are allowed, it is an agreed fact that their meals need to be as nourishing and protein-filled as possible. Similarly in the domain of literature — though they do read comics — it is accepted that children should not be bored or shocked or harrowed by what they read; that with their reading they should imbibe something of value; since each child reads only about six hundred books in the course of childhood, each book should nourish them in some way — with new ideas, insight, humour, or vocabulary.

Chapter Two

Warning: writing for children may not be as simple as you think

We will begin this chapter with an imaginary scene which takes place in the offices of the Department of Public Welfare, Children's Literature Section, Applications Board.

The selection board — cloaked, and concealed in black hoods with eye-slits, like the Spanish Inquisition — are sitting round a table, and a trembling postulant is brought before them, who has applied for permission to write children's stories.

'Your name is George Smith, and you wish to write a novel for children. What are your qualifications for making this application?'

'Well,' the trembling candidate stammers, 'I was a child myself, thirty years ago.'

'Who wasn't? What other reasons do you have to offer?' says the inquisitor.

'I've *got* two children. I — I tell them stories at bedtime.'

'That, again, is hardly unusual. What else?'

'I'm a teacher. I meet children every day.'

'Hmm. You may have half a point for that. You need to reach a total of twenty. What else?'

'I have a lot of spare time in the school holidays. I need the money.'

'No points. Go on.'

'I've *read* some of the kids' books that my children leave lying around the house. They're dead simple. I could knock off two or three just as good in a couple of months.'

'No points. Go on.'

'Well, I've always thought I'd like to try my hand at writing. Used to enjoy writing essays at school. But, these days, the adult novels seem so wild and way-out, I thought it would be easier to begin by breaking into the juvenile field first.'

'No points. Go on.'

'Well — as a matter of fact — I *know* a fellow in publishing. And he told me his firm is going to do a series of Easy-to-Read books, in simple vocabulary, aimed at ten-year-old reluctant readers —'

'Enough!' thunders the inquisitor. 'Take him away, drop him down the oubliette — but first, strangle him with his own typewriter ribbon!'

Now another candidate is brought in, a smiling little fellow, very sure of himself.

'What is your reason for wishing to write a children's novel?'

'You see,' says candidate number two. 'I work for this advertising agency; I have access to all the sociological surveys on kids' reading, I've run them through the computer, and I've come up with absolutely incontrovertible evidence that the most popular fictional character of this decade in the kids' market is a small brown furry talking male vegetarian animal, with a two-syllable name, who lives in the northern hemisphere. So I plan to write this book about a wombat named Walter —'

'Wombats live in the southern hemisphere.'

'The kids won't know that. And it doesn't matter. This is fantasy, see? The book is absolutely guaranteed to sell a hundred and fifty thousand on its first hardback printing. I'll have the storyline roughed out in two weeks —'

'Take him away!' shouts the grand inquisitor. 'Roast him in front of slowly burning market surveys.'

Then in comes a shabby fumbling figure who, in answer to the question, 'Why do you want to write a children's novel?' replies, 'Well, I don't exactly *want* to write one — I've written it. Here it is,' and he produces a scribbled bulky manuscript, adding vaguely, 'Mind you, I don't *know* that it's a children's book, I read it to my ninety-year-old aunt, and she liked it.'

'What's it about?'

'Well, I suppose you could say that it's about a bridge, a bridge over a fjord, a bridge that's beginning to rust. As well as that, it's about a trainee tea-taster, and an old lady who's fallen in love with a policeman, so she keeps setting off her burglar alarm — and there's a boy who's stolen a piece of turf from the middle of a famous football ground — and they all meet, going across the rusty bridge in a fog, and realise they have met before; I suppose you could say that the story was concerned with wishes and expectations — or, how hard it is to sell your soul to the devil if he doesn't want to *buy* your soul — well, anyway, it's a kind of ghost story.'

'The committee will read it,' says the grand inquisitor. 'And in the meantime you may have a thirty-day probationary period, working in the fiction incinerator, burning all the books about wombats named Walter. — Incidentally, should the committee decide that your book is worth having been written, what are your plans?'

'Plans, plans,' says the candidate, looking even vaguer than before. 'I haven't any plans, why?'

'Do you intend to write more books about rusting bridges?'

'Certainly not. I've finished the story about the rusty bridge. I've said all I have to say about rusty bridges.'

'But suppose your book is a best-seller. Suppose a publisher offered you a three-book contract, explaining that they were putting out a whole series on rusting bridges, aimed at the fourteen-to-sixteen age group — thirty-three to thirty-six thousand words each, which might also be the basis for a TV series of eighteen weekly half-hour programmes . . .'

. . . Well by this time you will have got the point I have been attempting to put across.

Why *do* people write for children?

Ideally, writing books for children should be a vocation. An enormous number of books for children have already been written — especially in the last thirty years. There are many good and strong arguments against becoming a children's writer just because it seems like a not-too-difficult way of making a bit of money.

True, a children's book is not so long or hard to write as an adult book. True, children's books, once afloat, sell more steadily than adult ones, which may never get past their first printing.

These are not in themselves sufficient reasons for entering the children's field. A child only reads six hundred books in the course of childhood. *All those six hundred have already been written.* There are hundreds of contemporary books for children — many of them first class. As well, there are all the classics; even if some of these are discarded, many should by no means be missed. With all of these, any child will be amply supplied.

So what need is there for you to write another children's book?

In view of this situation it is plain that nobody should enter into the field of children's literature merely because they have always had a vague urge to write something, and this seems a good way to get your hand in before tackling an adult book.

You should enter this field only because you have a strong urge to tell the kind of story *which you think children will enjoy*; preferably, because there is some particular story which is clamouring to be let out of your mind.

The greatest sin against children is to write books for them according to formula. That is as bad as selling them low-grade food, or shoes that are going to let in the wet.

What do I mean by formula? A glance through some children's book-review pages in national papers will show what I mean. Here are some of the plotlines: A pregnant girl tries to find her identity. A bear who doesn't like playing with other bears is asked to a party, and finally learns to socialise. Four children lose their dog but find him again thanks to a neighbour they had mistrusted. A dog learns to get on with a cat. Some children come to terms with some foreign neighbours. A boy learns to accept the fact that his mother is an alcoholic. Some children find some treasure.

Walter the wombat isn't in that list — but only *just* not.

You should not begin writing for children with the attitude that anything will do for children. Or think that a formula — like children finding treasure — or a message, however worthy — like a bear learning to make friends with other bears — is quite sufficient for the purpose, perfectly okay, and sure to find a publisher. Maybe it will. But it will not be literature. And the children who read it will be defrauded, as if they were being fed on skim milk.

Children's writers ought to dedicate themselves with the motto: only the best is good enough for children. Childhood is all too short now, and yearly becoming shorter as TV forces the pace of growing; children's reading-matter ought to have plenty of vitamins in it.

A children's writer should, ideally, be a dedicated semi-lunatic, a kind of poet with a marvellous idea, who, preferably, when not committing the marvellous idea to paper, does something else of a quite different kind, so as to acquire new and rich experience. Because no adult can live all the time in a child's world. It's not natural, and it's not wholesome. Teachers should do other things besides teaching; parents should get away from their children from time to time; children's writers need to stretch their brains and capacities in the same way, not to be continually making allowance for lesser experience.

14

> Literature is good for nothing if it is not admirably good. A
> writer . . . must make up his mind that he must not pursue
> authorship as a vocation with a trading determination to
> get rich by it. It is in the highest sense lawful for him to get
> as good a price as he honourably can for the best work he
> is capable of; but not for him to force or hurry his
> production, or even to do over again what has already
> been done . . .
>
> George Eliot, *Leaves from a Notebook.*

What should a children's writer write — and not write?

A children's book — a *good* children's book — is not something
that can be dashed off to schedule, turned off a production belt
like a piece of factory goods. It should not be anything with an axe
to grind, propaganda for something, a hidden sales-message. It
should not be perfunctory, meaningless, flat, coy, or second-rate.

Children have huge needs. There may be disastrous gaps in their
education, their environment, their upbringing. Not every child
lives in a happy, well-organised home or family. And any child,
however fortunate, may have some need which reading will help to
fill. Should writers feel any moral responsibility about this? Can
they do anything to fill these gaps?

Librarians — who tend, bless them, to look on books as a
commodity, rather as bakers do bread, or chemists cosmetics —
are apt to approach writers and say, 'Couldn't you write a book
about such-and-such, it would be so useful.'

This is putting the cart before the horse. Books should not be
written to order in this way. But of course it can do no harm for the
alert writer to keep scanning the scene, to be aware of
contemporary problems, if possible to study them at close quarters,
so that, perhaps unconsciously, his mind may begin to work and
churn and create ideas on current issues. A good children's writer
may be particularly well-equipped to do this. I have said that a
children's writer is a kind of lunatic or poet. Poets are the sensitive
points in a civilisation. They can't help being aware of problems,
and their writing can't help reflecting this awareness.

But beware! If you deliberately produce a book in order to point
out some wrong that needs righting, you will produce a tract. The
book will be journalism. It won't be nourishing.

15

The *story* is the main thing, and you should keep that in mind first, last, and all the time.

Beware, too, of over-simplification. There is a current fashion for suggesting that everything is very easy, if it is properly explained. Sex is simple, just a case of understanding about hormones and genes and contraception. Science is simple. Even old age and death are simple. If the sixth form are taken to visit a few geriatric wards, they will have it all taped in no time.

I can hardly state strongly enough what a mistake I think this is, to tell children that they will find a solution to every problem they are likely to encounter. First, it is a flat lie. Second, if they believe these optimistic assurances, they will end up as schizophrenics. Third, if they don't believe what they are told, it will make them mistrustful and cynical.

A writer lives, at best, in a state of astonishment.
William Sansom, *Blue Skies, Brown Studies*

So it is the writer's duty to demonstrate to children that the world is *not* a simple place. Far from it. The world is an infinitely rich, strange, confusing, wonderful, cruel, mysterious, beautiful, inexplicable riddle. We too are a riddle. We don't know where we come from or where we are going, we are surrounded by layers of meaning that we can only dimly apprehend, however much we try to learn.

And how much more enjoyable it is for children — how much more it accords with their own observations and instinctive certainties — to be told this, than to be told that the world is a flat, tidy, orderly place, with everything mapped out and accounted for by computer, with no unexplored regions left; that somewhere, neatly waiting, each person has an identity, like a parcel left at the post-office to be collected; that the naughty bear who doesn't like playing with other bears has only to be invited to a party, and he will soon change his ways.

> There, in the night, where none can spy
> All in my hunter's camp I lie,
> And play at books that I have read
> Till it is time to go to bed . . .
> And go to bed with backward looks
> At my dear land of story books.
> Robert Louis Stevenson,
A Child's Garden of Verses

Children need to get from the stories they read a sense of their own inner existence, and the archetypal links that connect them with the unexplored past; of the similarity in patterns between large and small, old and new; they need to receive something that extends beyond ordinary reality.

Stories ought not to be just little bits of fantasy that are used to wile away an idle hour; from the beginning of the human race stories have been used — by priests, by bards, by medicine men — as magic instruments of healing, of teaching, as a means of helping people come to terms with the fact that they continually have to face insoluble problems and unbearable realities.

A story should give a child some kind of glimpse or vision or key or intimation that things are not necessarily what they seem.

Of course it may be said, with some justice, that children don't need Coleridge's *Kubla Khan* or Poe's *Tales of Mystery and Imagination* to get such a feeling; they can get it from reading what seems to their parents the most abysmal trash — or, from a table with a blanket thrown over it.

But this is no argument against your trying to introduce into *your* story as much as you possibly can in the way of richness and interestingness and layers of meaning.

Your vision doesn't have to be beautiful. It just has to be your own — your own glimpse, your own angle. It may be a rusty bridge, a mousetrap, a dragon lost in a supermarket, a box of buttons, a wayside railway station. It may not be a thing, but a situation — a bird stuck inside an organ pipe, a crinolined lady in a revolving door, a person who tells his fortune every day by switching on the radio just long enough to hear one word.

What do you do then?

That must wait till the next chapter.

Chapter Three

The Different Age Groups

> From a five-year-old to a fifty-year-old is only a step, but from a newborn infant to a five-year-old is a terrifying distance.
>
> Tolstoy

Publishers, booksellers, teachers, librarians, and parents would all of them like to split children up into age groups so that shelves can be allocated in libraries and bookshops 'for the eight to ten age group'; so that reading lists and publishers' catalogues can be neatly set out, so that parents can march into a bookshop and demand 'a book for my nine-year-old' and emerge with the triumphant certainty that they have exactly the right article.

Of course this is nonsense. You would not go into a bookshop and ask for a novel 'for my forty-year-old husband' or 'my thirty-five-year-old wife.' Children, like adults, vary in their tastes and reading habits.

The young Brontes, at twelve and under, read Blackwoods Magazine:

> Nobody could think speak or write of anything but the catholic question . . . with what eagerness papa tore off the cover and how we all gathered round him.
>
> Charlotte Bronte, *Tales of the Islanders.*

They also read Aesop's *Fables,* Byron's works, Goldsmith's *History of Rome,* and *The Arabian Nights' Entertainments.*

The poet Yeats, on the other hand, was a very backward reader; his family began to think he must be mentally deficient.

> At six years old I remember to have read *Belisarius, Robinson Crusoe,* and Philip Quarles; and then I found the *Arabian Nights' Entertainments . . .* My father found out the effect which these books had produced, and burnt them.
>
> Samuel Taylor Coleridge, *Letter to Poole,* 1797.

Eighteen-year-old college students read C. S. Lewis's Narnia books, ten-year-olds gobble down H. G. Wells's short stories or William Golding's *Lord of the Flies.* It is impossible to predict who will read what. 'What age group do you write for?' is a question frequently asked of children's writers, and most of them tend to reply, 'My own age.'

However, since some form of division and classification must be found for the purpose of the present guide, we will employ rough-and-ready tactics, grouping readers into Small, Medium, and Large.

The Small group will be held to comprehend children who can't yet read themselves, or who have only recently acquired the art, say three to eight.

Medium age, the most interesting group, extends from children who have begun to read to themselves for pleasure, up to the age when they cease to want their reading-matter illustrated, and begin to borrow books from the adult library.

Large. This group is having to digest a lot of compulsory reading for its O and A levels, so reading for pleasure may have begun to taper off. At this stage the sexes tend to veer away from one another: girls continue to enjoy fantasy and romance, the majority of boys move towards non-fiction, and for their fiction push on into the world of adult novels, Graham Greene, Golding, D. H. Lawrence, Waugh, and the whole world of thrillers and spy stories, teen and pop magazines and soft porn.

To try and fill the gap caused by the cleavage, a thing called the teenage novel has been invented. This will be discussed in a later chapter.

Small Children's Books

The smallest child needs no text at all, and is happy simply to gaze at pictures, whether or not they tell a story. There is no reason why they should not. *Rosie's Walk* by Pat Hutchins is a classically simple and winning example of the story told entirely in pictures:

the innocent, carefree hen wandering through the farmyard and the wily fox in pursuit of her, foiled at every point by natural events, while the hen remains serenely unaware of her danger.

Basic picture-books have been around for a long time, since Comenius's *Orbis Pictus* in 1659. There have been animal books, with pictures more, or less, accurate, Happy Families books, natural history books, farm books, and, more recently, car, plane, ship and space books, each with a picture to each page.

But this kind of book is initiated by the artist, whereas it is to be assumed that you, the writer, are not thinking of a book from the pictorial angle, but intend each page to carry some text, however minimal.

The most minimal of all is, of course, the alphabet book. Alphabet books come in every sort — zoo, household, flower, avocational, or simply nonsense.

My advice, unless you have a stunningly original idea and have thought it through from A to Z, including X, is to avoid alphabets; beginners tend to make for them, publishers tend to be overloaded, and the usual reaction is to throw up their hands and cry, 'Not *another* alphabet book . . .'

Very small children's books should, naturally, be written with the question of illustration well to the front of your mind. Pick a theme that illustrates easily and gracefully. Nobody is going to be happy if your storyline concerns complicated machinery, or abstract mental concepts, or highly elaborate scenes, or anything that will be difficult to put across visually. And muddled or pretentious pictures can destroy a text.

The visual and verbal components of a small child's story are of equal importance and should complement and reinforce each other. Often pictures and text are by the same hand. It would be impossible to think of Beatrix Potter's stories without her own illustrations; Kathleen Hale's *Orlando* books, Edward Ardizzone's *Little Tim* series, Kipling's illustrations to the *Just-So Stories,* de Brunhoff's Babar all have the same inevitability; and in the same way Pooh has come to be wedded to the E. H. Shepard illustrations as indissolubly as Alice to Tenniel because of the close rapport between author and illustrator.

So before you even begin your small child's book, the question of illustration has to be thought about: will it be done by you or somebody else?

That being decided one way or the other (some pros and cons will be dealt with in a later chapter) you come to your story.

What should it be about?

> We should address ourselves to those faculties in a child's mind which are first awakened by nature, and consequently first admit of cultivation, that is to say the memory and the imagination.
>
> Samuel Taylor Coleridge, *The Education of Children*

If you are proposing to write a book for very small children, the likelihood is that you yourself have a child in this age group. Adult writers such as T. H. White, Thackeray, Tolkien, are sometimes moved to write fantasies which will be read by medium-size children or teenagers, because they themselves retain a kind of hot line back to the imaginative world of childhood; but it is rare for an adult suddenly to embark on a *tiny* child's story without the immediate stimulus of an actual nursery-age child somewhere close at hand.

In the unlikely event that you are planning to write a small child's book *without* being in frequent contact with someone in this age group, you must take pains to put yourself in contact with one, or several.

Visit friends with kindergarten-age children, spend time playing with them, sit with them at meal times, watch the bedtime ritual, accompany them to the beach, sing to them, play with them, take them for walks. Listen to their speech rhythms, ponder their vocabularies. This sounds elementary sense, doesn't it? Nobody ever wrote a really good book for small children on a basis of merely distant acquaintance with them. Yet it is remarkable how many aspirant writers launch confidently into this field without that elementary experience. Presumably they think that, because there needs to be very little text on each page, the writing of such a book must be quick and easy.

Because there are very few words on each page, their importance is paramount; as much frenzy and deliberation may go into the selection of half a dozen words as into a political manifesto. A sonnet is harder than a saga. Guinness is Good For You probably took a year to compose. The cat sat on the mat may have given equal trouble.

Easy writing's curst hard reading.

Sheridan, *Clio's Protest*

21

Before you decide to write your small-child's story, take time to observe the small child and discover where its interests lie. Don't just go to the nearest bookstore and study the picture-books there — they may not be a good guide.

> I achieved Miss Wardley's approval by writing long faked essays on the lives and habits of otters. I'd never seen an otter, or even gone to look for one, but the essays took her in.
>
> Laurie Lee, *Cider With Rosie.*

A huge percentage of small-children's books are about animals. It seems, for the last century, to have become a natural assumption that all small children must automatically be interested in the animal kingdom, preferably its furry representatives. Bill the bear, Oswald the otter, Fred the fox, Sam the squirrel — they, or their cousins, are all there on the picture-book shelf.

But are all small children really interested to this degree?

Statistics show that most children in the western world are now reared in urban surroundings. Books about Susan the seal may look very attractive, but are they related in any way to the children's day-to-day existence? They are a legacy from when it was logical to follow the precept of Coleridge quoted above and educate children's faculties by awakening them to nature, which, in those days, was all around. Even during the life of our grandparents animals made natural subjects for nursery stories. Now it is no longer so.

If you are thinking about writing the life of Bessie the badger, maybe you should think again? Besides, there are plenty of animal stories already in existence — Peter Rabbit, Little Grey Rabbit, *Watership Down* are firmly established on the rabbit shelf. Perhaps you can make a contribution to children's literature without adding Deb the donkey. How often do small children see a donkey?

I am not saying there is no room for a new, truly imaginative, sympathetic and original animal story. All I wish to suggest is that you begin by looking closer to your audience.

What are small children's primary interests and occupations? Food, clothes, the process of getting up, going to bed, bathtime, walks, visits to shops, riding on buses, watching parental activities. Unlimited imaginative material here for stories!

Heaven lies around us in our infancy.

William Wordsworth, *Ode, Intimations of Immortality*

Consider the simple process of making toast — a ritual which occurs in ninety-nine households out of a hundred several times a week, if not daily, in our civilisation. From the small child's viewpoint there must be something magical about the transformation: the severance of a thin, flabby white slice from a thick soft block of bread, and its transition (by means of whatever process, grill, toaster, or fork) into a hot crisp delicacy.

There is excellent substance for fiction here, and the same is true of innumerable other household activities.

Remember how minutely observant and noticing small children are. It is their paramount quality. And the acuteness of their observation will be your ally; day after day they have watched the routine of toast-making (or whatever you have chosen) with the serious, engrossed attention which is given by adults only to major athletics or scientific experiments. If you talk to four-year-olds about toast, you are talking to an audience of aficionados, professional experts.

Small children notice objects or happenings *on their own level.* I mean that literally. A friend of mine, taking her pre-school children to Paris, found that the foreign differences and peculiarities which excited their interest were all at knee-level or lower: advertisements and graffiti on walls of pissoirs, drain grating patterns, doorsteps, cobbles, foreign cigarette packets, objects in gutters. Large structures like the Eiffel Tower were too far away for their attention; they probably had not yet noticed the Post Office Tower back at home.

If, when addressing small children, you choose a subject that lies within their range of experience, you are giving yourself a head start. And you can be just as imaginative about toast as about Thomas the turtle.

There must always be exceptions, naturally. If you really want to write about Paul the puma, go ahead. The story you want to write is always better than the one you feel you ought to write.

But it seems a pity to waste the resources that lie so close at hand.

Stairs, cupboards, blankets, sinks, ovens, soap, shoes, clocks, knitting, paper-bags — all these can be full of mystery, excitement, and beauty. Why not turn them to account?

23

> The gingham dog and the calico cat
> Side by side on the table sat . . .
> Eugene Field, *The Duel, Poems of Childhood*

Toys, of course, are a topic of continuous imaginative activity for small children. Many toys have become famous and given rise to sagas. Pooh, Piglet, Raggedy Ann, Paddington . . . Innumerable novels have been written about dolls, marionettes such as Pinocchio, dolls' houses, building bricks, stuffed animals. Your own child may have some battered beloved companion which has already become the focus of household legend, and which you feel deserves to be immortalised in the footsteps of Sooty or Thomas the Tank Engine. But think carefully about this. There are hazards here. Because the saga delights your own family, are you sure it is potent enough to charm the world? Toys, moreover, tend to go out of fashion fast; I remember in my childhood being baffled by tales of golliwogs, already a rarity, and things called Dismal Desmonds, which had wholly ceased to exist. So choose something fairly basic. Another hazard, one which A. A. Milne did not wholly escape, is that of cuteness or archness. So write with care.

Writers unacquainted with the genre tend to believe that *all* small children's books must, *ipso facto,* be cute. This is a gross error. Small children are the most serious students in the human race. They have to be. They are learning something every minute of the daylight hours, at a faster pace and over a wider range of knowledge than they will ever need to again. Cuteness has no place in their experience. Cuteness, if it is found in small children's books, has been put there to catch the attention of the adults, and that is a serious sin. Study the work of Maurice Sendak, Quentin Blake, John Burningham. You will find no cuteness there.

When you write for children you should be writing with a single mind and voice. Never be arch, never be coy. Tell your story plainly and roundly.

The plot of a small children's book need not be elaborate. A quest pursued to its end, a task achieved, a hazard overcome, all make good storylines. Piaget holds that small children do not recognise chance or coincidence; they believe the world to be run by moral laws; so your chain of causality should be a direct one.

Over the last ten to twelve years there has grown up a fashion for books ostensibly aimed at the nursery age group, but which are really coffee-table books, aimed at their parents — glossy, beautifully, lavishly, elaborately, sometimes grotesquely illustrated, costing considerably more than the average parent is prepared to spend on a book to be battered by a four-year-old. The text is sophisticated, often in verse. You will find them in all large bookstores. If you are interested in writing this kind of text, it must be said that there appears to be a steady demand for them, but they are not really children's books.

> I would follow her eyes — how blue! — as they moved across the page, and I could always tell when she tried to skip anything. I would stop her then, and insist on hearing every word.
>
> James Kirkup, *The Only Child.*

The *rhythm* of a small child's story is tremendously important. A large proportion of them will be read aloud, not once, but hundreds of times, over and over and over.

Consider this agreeable passage from Beatrix Potter's Tom Kitten: 'The three Puddle Ducks came along the hard high road marching one behind the other . . . pit pat paddle pat, pit pat waddle pat.' My daughter absolutely adored that sentence, it sent her into ecstasies of laughter every time. 'Read it again, Ma,' she'd cry, 'Read it *again!*'

> There was a ritual about them [The Just So Stories], each phrase having its special intonation which had to be exactly the same each time.
>
> Angela Thirkell, *Three Houses*

Kipling's *Just So Stories* are a superlative example of well-used rhythm. The words and phrases swing along, carrying the reader with them:

> He ran through the desert; he ran through the mountains; he ran through the salt-pans; he ran through the reed-beds; he ran through the blue-gums; he ran through the spinifex; he ran till his front legs ached.
> He had to!
>
> Rudyard Kipling, *Old Man Kangaroo,*
> from *The Just So Stories.*

It is as much of a pleasure (luckily) to read those lines for the hundredth time as for the first.

They are also an example of the fact that unfamiliar words may safely be introduced into a text for small children.

> There were still many words, even in the first pages of that simple primer, she could not decipher; but she could skip those and still make sense of the whole.
>
> Flora Thompson, *Lark Rise to Candleford.*

It is a fallacy that unfamiliar words will discourage children from reading. On the contrary, they may be a particular pleasure. The blue-gums and the spinifex gave special quality to the story of Old Man Kangaroo for me when I heard it first at age three; and the fact that I did not know what spinifex was only added to the incantatory quality of the whole.

As a matter of fact, I still don't know what spinifex is. (It is not in the Concise O.E.D. But I have managed to get along without the knowledge.)

Provided you keep your *sentences* short and rhythmic, your vocabulary may be quite rich. Experts differ diametrically (as experts always do) about whether language in early books should be kept to a basic vocabulary or not; so you may as well please yourself (and the children).

Educationalists have suddenly discovered (in 1981) that it is a Good Thing for parents to read aloud to children, so, if your book is published, remember that parents, too, will bless you if the lines fall trippingly off the tongue.

> Cats here, cats there, cats and kittens everywhere. Hundreds of cats, thousands of cats, millions and billions and trillions of cats.
>
> Wanda Gag, *Millions of Cats*

Keep the rhythm moving, keep the sense clear, and you'll keep the readers happy:

> If I were a cassowary
> On the plains of Timbuctoo
> I would eat a missionary
> Cassock, bands, and hymn-book too.
>
> Bishop Samuel Wilberforce, *Impromptu Verse*

Of course if you want to try your hand at a basic-vocabulary story, no one is stopping you.

An American publisher once invited me to contribute a story of this kind to a series they were compiling, and they sent me the vocabulary and instructions about grammar — no past tenses were allowed, for instance, if the verb changed its form, think to thought, or go to went.

I quote from their word-list: Apple, around, aunt, automobile, bad, bear, big, bigger, biggest, bluebird, bow-wow, Christmas, cookie, dark, doll, dream, drive, electric, fairy, fight, football, goldfish, grandma, grandpa, grandma's, grandpa's (for some reason grandma and grandpa were the only proper nouns allowed the genitive case, which shows a nice respect for old age) hurt, jack-o-lantern, lovely, mind, milk, much, my, nickel, newspaper, park, pumpkin, road, run, sell, space, telephone, ticket, tie, train, trip, truck, turkey, wanted, woman, yes, yours, yesterday, zoo.

(To an English ear this list seems to proffer the whole American way of life in an amazingly condensed packet.) But when it came to writing stories in this vocabulary, with all its restrictions, I found myself unable to do so.

English educational publishers have produced their own word-lists and will supply them to aspirant writers, but this kind of writing is hedged about with difficulties; a friend of mine worked on some limited-vocabulary stories for such a publisher and grew discouraged because when, despite the cramping conditions, she did manage to produce lively and inventive stories, each one had to be processed, about three times over, by a committee of experts, who raised objections to any but the dullest and flattest language.

I once had an idea for doing basic-vocabulary stories for non-literate prison inmates, following the style of shorthand primers:

'Has Dan got a Hot Rod?
No, but Tom has a Hot Car.
Did Ned win a Van off the Man?
No, but Tim can do a Ton. Is a Ton a lot? A Ton is not a lot.
Run, Tom, run. I saw a Cop pop out of the Pub.
Why is Nan in the Can?
She got her Axe to fix the tax Man.'

But somehow this never got off the ground; I could not interest any publisher in the idea.

My advice, on the whole, is to avoid limited vocabulary stories, and, if you have a good idea for a small children's book, write it regardless of vocabulary in the best way you can.

Remember that very small children are the equivalent of Stone Age Man. Since they cannot yet read for themselves — or are just on the brink — they need the texts they hear to be *immediately memorable,* so that, when they are alone in cot or playpen, they can summon up the pleasure once more for themselves. Rhythmic words have a remarkably solacing effect in trouble, too.

27

Once my son fell and hurt himself. 'What'll I do to make it better?' I asked. 'Sing dilly dilly Carmen,' he sobbed. '*Dilly dilly Carmen?*' 'Dilly dilly Carmen be killed.'

Perhaps somebody should consider the operatic possibilities of *Mrs Bond.*

Bear in mind such examples as these:

I'll *huff* and I'll *puff,* and I'll *blow* your house down.
Piggy won't get over the *stile,* and *I* shan't get home *tonight.*
Still she sat, and *still* she span, and *still* she wished for *com*pany.

The lilt of a story, for the reading parent with small child on lap, is very close to the earlier, embryonic, or cradle-rocking rhythms.

Many small children's books now are beautifully produced and written with every care in regard to literary and psychological considerations — but they don't win their way to the readers' hearts simply because they have neglected the crucially important matter of rhythm.

Child! do not throw this book about.
Hilaire Belloc, *Cautionary Tales for Children*

You may decide that the small child's story is not your metier. Shortness of length, and the need for illustrations, render it too limiting for you. (Note: I do not speak of limitation of *subject-matter.* Any subject that can be agreeably illustrated and tunefully narrated may provide subject-matter for a small child's story if deployed with the right mix of poetry and straightforwardness).

You, however, have decided to set your sights on the next age-group, the Medium-size child. And this may be a wise decision. Publishers are bombarded with mss. of small children's stories, since the shortness of length (thirty pages is the average) makes such a book seem an attractively easy proposition for beginners.

A full-length novel offers more challenge. Also, since the flow of such novels into publishers' offices is not so large, merit may stand out more clearly. And, for the editor, it is easier to judge a new writer's potential in a manuscript of 40,000 to 60,000 words than one of five hundred to a thousand.

If you are aiming at the Medium age group, you will be in good company. The medium child's novel — addressing, very roughly, the age range from nine to fourteen — is what most people are thinking about when they refer to a children's book.

This category encompasses all the great works of children's literature: Molesworth, Alcott, Kipling, Grahame, Hodgson Burnett, Nesbit, Mark Twain, John Masefield, Walter de la Mare, Arthur Ransome, Hugh Lofting, T. H. White, Buchan, Erich Kastner, Rosemary Sutcliff, C. S. Lewis, Tolkien, Alan Garner, William Mayne, E. B. White, Leon Garfield, George Selden, Russell Hoban, Philippa Pearce — to name only a handful.

(If many of the above names mean nothing to you, may I suggest here that you step round to your local library and take pains to read at least one book by most of the writers listed. I am not suggesting that you should repeat what they have done. But — firstly, it may be that the book you are contemplating has already been written. Better make certain that this is not so. Secondly, no area of creative endeavour should be entered without (a) a command of basic abilities and requirements, and (b) an acquaintance with the masters.

We assume that your grammar, vocabulary, and syntax are above reproach. You would not otherwise be proposing to write for children, whose reading forms such an important part of their education.

But if you have only a small or minimal knowledge of the great children's books written in the last hundred years, now is the moment to enlarge it.

They who have the skill
To manage books and things, and make them act
On infant minds.
                    William Wordsworth, *The Prelude*

What do you want to write *about* — having decided that you fulfil the above requirements?

For a discussion of this, you must turn to the next chapter.

Chapter Four

Novels for Children of Medium Age

> Oh, give us once again the wishing-cap
> Of Fortunatus, and the invisible coat
> Of Jack the Giant-Killer, Robin Hood
> And Sabra in the forest with St. George!
> The child whose love is here at least, doth reap
> One precious gain, that he forgets himself.
> William Wordsworth, *The Prelude*

The range of subject-matter in the novel for children of medium age, nine to fourteen, is very wide. (If you have followed the reading advice given at the end of the last chapter, you will know this already.)

Domestic, school stories, adventure, whether at home or in foreign lands, sea stories, theatre, ballet, circus, film settings, war, historical, science fiction, fantasy, are only some of the many possibilities. This is what makes this age group so attractive. And there are many areas which fall into no sort of classification at all. Where would you put Kastner's *Emil and the Detectives?* Or Natalie Babbitt's *Tuck Everlasting?* Or George Selden's *A Cricket in Times Square?* Or Frances Hodgson Burnett's *The Secret Garden?* Works of genius cannot be tucked neatly into slots.

What do you want to write about?

Of course — as I said in Chapter Two — it is to be hoped that you are not just vaguely casting around for some idea which might, perhaps, do; but already have your idea slotted into your creative mechanism, and what you need is advice about how to make the most of it.

One thing to keep in mind is that few, very few, really good works of art are produced in a hurry. No doubt Picasso dashed off magnificent drawings at breakneck speed, Haydn shot out symphonies like bullets, Keats produced his greatest masterpieces in a molten flood — but these were men of genius, and, furthermore, had a mass of previous work and experience as a base.

The average novel of 40,000 to 60,000 words — which is the general length of a children's book — takes approximately six to nine months to write.

No doubt Enid Blyton and Edgar Wallace produced a book a week. But they, like Haydn and Picasso, worked on a basis of long professional experience; and both were assisted by secretaries and research staff. Nor can they be considered ideal models to emulate. Wallace's style was sadly slipshod, and Blyton used the same plot over and over.

So accustom yourself to the prospect that your book is going to take most of a year — at least six months' planning and six months' writing. It may be longer, depending on the number of hours' work you can give to it daily.

Note that I said *daily*.

Writing Routine

It is to be assumed, since you are only just at the point of considering writing a children's novel, that you already have some other occupation — you are a teacher, a functioning parent, work in office or factory, or combine several of these pursuits. Your book may need to be written in scarce spare time, in the evening or at night. It may be hard to find regular time for writing.

Nevertheless you *must* find it. Regularity is a fundamental necessity of good writing; especially good writing for children. Offbeat or *avant garde* works may be produced spasmodically or unsystematically, but a children's book needs a strong, consistent style, and the only way to achieve this is by disciplined. regular output.

My first literary agent, Jean LeRoy (who wrote an excellent little guide to magazine and serial authorship, *Sell Them a Story,* published by Constable in 1954) urged all the writers whose work she handled, and some were very prestigious, to make a habit of writing at least six pages a day. 'You *must* keep it flowing,' was her maxim, 'or it will dry up.' As cows need milking, sweetpeas need picking, so writers must continually exercise their mental muscles by a daily stint. Jean LeRoy also said that your spare time will always magically expand to contain what you need to do in it; the pocket of time, she called it. This I have found to be true.

Regular work on a novel is absolutely essential. The plot and characters may be well established in your mind. But it is a constant battle to ensure that they are not swamped with other, personal preoccupations. Keep them to the *front* of your mind by conscious effort. Use odd moments during the day — while brushing your teeth, standing in the queue at the post office, riding on a bus, peeling potatoes, washing socks — to work at your story, to brood about the characters, attack problems and find solutions. This will take much discipline. Your friends and family won't enjoy it. No one ever said that writing was an easy life. Sometimes you have to force your mind to address itself to a difficulty — it feels like pushing an elephant up Mount Everest. But it is worth the effort.

Assemble your story in your mind each night just before falling asleep. Very, very often dreams or your subconscious will solve some problem for you during the night.

If you do not work at your story every day, or at least devote some time to conscious planning and thinking — then the struggle to get back into it after each interval away from it will be proportionately harder and more painful depending on the length of the gap. You may find that you have to waste days and days getting back into the mood, picking up the thread, rediscovering the voice. Pages and pages of writing may have to be discarded.

Voice

Each book has its own. Had you noticed that?

Consider a few examples:

> Morgraunt was before him, and of Morgraunt all the country spoke in a whisper. It was far, it was deep, it was dark as night, haunted with the waving of perpetual woods; it lay between the mountains and the sea, a mystery as inviolate as either.
>
> Maurice Hewlett, *The Forest Lovers*

> Once, on a dark winter's day, when the yellow fog hung so thick and heavy in the streets of London that the lamps were lighted and the shop windows blazed with gas as they do at night, an odd-looking little girl sat in a cab with her father, and was driven rather slowly through the big thoroughfares.
>
> Frances Hodgson Burnett, *A Little Princess*

And now it appeared again, vague, yet very awful, in the dim twilight the sun had left behind him. But just before it reached him, down from its four long legs it dropped, flat on the ground, and came crawling towards him, wagging a huge tail as it came.

George Macdonald, The Princess and Curdie

Why couldn't you have picked out a name with a little personality? I might as well write letters to Dear Hitching-Post or Dear Clothes-Prop. I have been thinking about you a great deal this summer . . . It seems as though I belonged to somebody now, and it's a very comfortable sensation.

Jean Webster, Daddy-Long-Legs

Each of those passages has a completely unmistakable voice. It is not so much a case of style — an author may vary his style from book to book, depending on the audience he is addressing, but nonetheless his basic style will remain unchanged.

But the voice of each book is unique. Maurice Hewlett adopted a heroic voice for *The Forest Lovers,* a tale of romance and chivalry. Jean Webster, adopting the form of letters, took the voice of her college-girl heroine as narrator. In each case the voice is so individual that, merely from one snippet of prose, a reader familiar with them can summon up the flavour of the whole book.

If you have found a voice for your book, even if the plot and characters are still at the embryonic stage of development, your battle is half won already. Nothing encourages the flow of a story so much as the discovery of the voice in which it is to be told. I once sat down and began a book with the lines, 'It was dusk — winter dusk. Snow lay white and shining over the pleated hills . . .' In those fourteen words I had already fixed the whole mood and atmosphere of the story so firmly that, though the book they began was interrupted after three chapters by outside circumstances, and not recommenced until after a gap of seven years, when I took it up again, I had not the slightest difficulty in going on from where I had left off.

Your Imaginary Reader

Voice, of course, has a strong connection with your imaginary reader.

Almost every writer has an ideal reader in mind — who may, of course, vary from book to book. Kipling, when writing the *Just So Stories,* was talking to his daughter Josephine. A. A. Milne was writing for Christopher Robin. Charlotte M. Yonge wrote all her books for her father. (A pity, on the whole.) You, perhaps, are writing for your child, or children. This is an excellent thing. The imaginary reader helps the writer to preserve his single voice — every sentence is aimed at that specific ear, and this gives the work unity and consistency.

If you *don't* have any imaginary reader in mind, perhaps you should consider selecting one? Yourself at age twelve? Your cat? Your old English teacher? Your niece?

When I worked on a short-story magazine, we invented, for editorial purposes, our Average Reader, whom we called Uncle Arthur: a retired bank manager, fond of animals and adventure stories, rather conservative, who played golf, drank beer, and travelled a great deal on trains. In any case of editorial doubt — was a story too tough, too sentimental, too fantastic, too silly? — if the staff could not agree, the matter was referred to Uncle Arthur, who seldom failed to come up with a firm decision.

A child can identify with adult characters — but only if they are sympathetically drawn and simple enough.
E. W. Hildick, *Children and Fiction*

You have found the voice in which you want your book to be told. Now you have the flavour and feeling of the book and some idea of its theme.

Your Central Character

Who is your central character to be?

This may be an idle question. Perhaps the whole theme is so involved and intermeshed with the main character that there is no doubt — one cannot be thought of without the other. But suppose this is not the case. Suppose (for instance) you wish to write a nostalgic melancholy book about the withdrawal of the last Roman garrisons from Britain in A.D.442; after four hundred years of affluence and civilisation, nothing but dark and terror lies ahead. You intend to draw a parallel with the present period. You know a sufficient amount of background information so that you can write comfortably without constant recourse to reference books — but how do you pick your main character? Are there any rules about it?

Well, no, there are not. It is a fallacy that all stories for children must be written *about* children. After all, the heroes of folk tales and legends are mostly adult — or they grow to adulthood in the course of the saga. Robin Hood, King Arthur, Cuchulain, Theseus, the three Musketeers, Hereward, Davy Crockett, Batman, Superman, Dr Who, are all grown up. (It must be a source of regret to women's lib that there are so few female hero-figures, but there are *some:* Artemis, Joan of Arc, Boadicea, and maybe Florence Nightingale?)

So your main figure may be child or adult, male or female, the choice is entirely up to you. Indeed, theoretically, I see no reason why the hero should not be an elderly person; it would be slightly more uphill work to make a child reader empathise with such a hero but if he has good relations with the young — like Socrates for instance — and is lovable, interesting, well-invented, there seems no reason why readers should not participate in his problems and struggles. Or, of course, your main character can be an animal. (Piaget, by the way, says that if there are no children in a story, the child reader will identify with animals. But if there are neither children nor animals, presumably he does the best he can with grown-ups.)

Now you have your main character, or group of characters.

If you decide on children, perhaps a family, and have several of them, do, for heaven's sake, try to avoid referring to them as 'the children' all the time. For some reason it gives a strangely patronising, nineteenth century flavour to a piece of writing; as if children were not individuals in themselves, but a kind of mass product. After all, you would not refer to the other characters as 'the adults.'

Story-telling or Describing

> The last thing one settles in writing a book is what one should put in first.
>
> Pascal, *Pensées* 1670

Before plunging in, it might be advisable to re-examine *why* you have an urge to write. (We assume that you have, or you would not be proposing to write this children's book. If you *don't* really enjoy writing, and are just doing it for the extra income you hope it will bring, now is the time to abandon the whole project and turn to some other source of revenue.)

Fine. You are sure that you enjoy writing. Now read the following two passages and decide which of them you would prefer to have written.

It was a curious sight — the boy with the knife that shone in the low sunlight as it sifted through the upper branches, and the silent Pack with their red coats all aflame, huddling and following below . . .

'Take thy tail,' said Mowgli . . . 'And follow now — to the death.'

He had slipped down the tree-trunk, and headed like the wind, in bare feet, for the Bee Rocks.

Rudyard Kipling, *Red Dog* from *The Two Jungle Books*

This room had heavy dark red stuff curtains — the colour that blood would not make a stain on — with coarse lace curtains inside . . . The fireplace had shavings and tinsel in it. There was a very varnished mahogany chiffonier, or sideboard, with a lock that wouldn't act. There were hard chairs — far too many of them — with crochet antimacassars slipping off their seats, all of which sloped the wrong way. The table wore a cloth of a cruel green colour with a yellow chain-stitch pattern round it. Then there was a mantel-board with maroon plush and wool fringe that did not match the plush; a dreary clock like a black marble tomb . . . And there were painted glass vases that never had any flowers in, and a painted tambourine that no one ever played, and painted brackets with nothing on them . . . There were — but I cannot dwell longer on this painful picture.

E. Nesbit, *The Story of the Amulet*

Novel writing has to be a combination of two urges, the urge to tell a story, and the simple yearning to *describe*. The second is a more natural attribute and is with most of us from childhood on; the first, to some degree, must be learned.

The art of story-telling is one that nearly everybody can acquire, if they think it worthwhile and set themselves to the task — in the same way that any other technique, rollerskating, or tennis, or pastry-making, can also be learned.

And story-telling certainly must be learned if you want to write a children's novel, for if you do nothing but describe (as E. Nesbit does in the passage quoted above) although it may be a pleasure to you, and to some of your readers, others will automatically skip all your best descriptions, and the plot will creep at a snail's pace.

As a matter of fact, very often, at the end of a book, it is the descriptions that the reader remembers and may even go back to read again: the case with the silver skates, in *Hans Brinker*; the Christmas presents that Judy bought herself, in *Daddy Long-Legs*; the infant wedding in *The Chaplet of Pearls*. But the *story* is what got the reader to the end of the book in the first place; if the story had not held him he would have put the book back on the shelf.

If you enjoy describing, you are an essayist; if the well-turned phrase gives you pleasure, you may be a poet; but if what interests you is *situations,* and the actions and behaviour of people in those situations, then you are a story-teller.

> A man may write at any time if he will set himself doggedly to it.
>
> Samuel Johnson,
> *Boswell's Journal of a Tour to the Hebrides*

Assembling your Material; Getting Started

You are making good progress. You have the flavour of your book, you feel fairly sure that you can tell your story, and the image of your central character has settled in your mind; how do you get started?

First, assemble all your material. Keep a large folder, and a notebook. Into the folder put any bits of relevant background information, and results of research, newspaper cuttings, scribbled ideas on envelopes, photographs that have reminded you of your characters, quotations, and memos to yourself. Into the notebook — which you carry with you *everywhere* — to meals, on walks, to the office, take it with you into the bathroom, slip it under your pillow at night — into this notebook, scribble all the ideas that may arise at any time, relative to your story.

'Uncle Thaddeus caught his foot in a badger trap when young.'

'Delia has a mad passion for marshmallows.'

'He didn't *know* that she had posted the letter. That was why he was out looking for Simon.'

In the folder, have a separate sheet of paper for each character in your story, and write down on this, as they come up, all these bits of description, past history, and salient features. So that by the time you start to write, you have a fairly complete portrait of each main figure. These may not actually be used when you come to writing your story, but *you* have got to know them. If your villain is colour-blind, if your hero fell into a mudbank at age three, if old Mr Gibson knows the complete works of Homer by heart . . . put it all down. Whether they are left- or right-handed, how they speak, what they dream about . . . put it down.

When you have assembled enough of this material, which will begin to look like a rook's nest; then you can think about making a schema, or chart.

Some writers never bother to do this. They just let the story flow with them as it will, like a river. They have a vague awareness that the hero is going to stow away on a Roman galley, float round the coast of Gaul, perhaps be discovered and put ashore; meanwhile his old father, back at home, is having a dreadful time with the barbarians arriving . . . But that is all they need to know in order to start off.

Other writers (of whom I am one) need to have a neatly drawn chart, with a large square for each chapter, and the main action therein carefully set out.

(1) Lucius discovers he isn't really Antoninus' son. Begs to be allowed to go with Vertumnus. Refused. Information about terrifying barbarians on the way. Death of old Portia. Romans packing up. Describe Fishbourne Palace as luxury goods removed; cuts to barbarians travelling through Ashdown Forest murdering & plundering . . . etc etc.

I, personally, can't feel comfortable about beginning a book unless I have this chart (which is the product of some months of thought) quite fully set out.

In the event, almost always, after I have been at work for a while, I start to diverge from the chart; more incidents come into each chapter than I first arranged for, and chapters have to be split in two; minor characters grow and play a larger part than had been expected; but the general shape and structure remains as originally planned.

This planning a book is the hardest work of all; you need all your mental muscles in good fettle for it; besides an atmosphere that is fairly free from distraction. Planning is a very condensed operation.

What can be done to hasten the creative process?

Decide which is your best time of day. In the morning, just after you wake? In your bath at night? Walking to work? Make use of that time, don't waste it.

Is there any activity that will assist thought? I find mowing the lawn good, or riding in a train (not car driving, you have to concentrate too hard on the traffic). Coleridge took laudanum, Kipling sat at his desk and sharpened all his pencils, Michael Gilbert, who writes excellent thrillers, goes for a walk downhill, Turgenev sat with his feet in a bucket of hot water.

If you can train your subconscious to co-operate in this way, so much the better; if not, the only thing is to wait patiently; trying to hurry a plot can be a fatal mistake and lead to trouble later. Sometimes it will move along so far and no further; a minor-seeming but insuperable snag arises and the mind baulks like a horse refusing a jump. You may patiently bring the horse back to the jump again and again; but if you leave it a little, or sleep on it, as likely as not the problem will, in the end, solve itself; you return to find the horse has flown the jump while your back was turned. During the waiting-period, try to tackle some other part of the story so as to distract yourself.

Once you have the nucleus of a story in your mind — like a submerged wreck sticking out of the water — you will often find that other pieces of material become attracted and cling to it; in fact, once your story is under way, you will be surprised how many elements of your every-day experience seem to be related to your work.

For a discussion of plots and story-planning, turn to the next chapter.

Chapter Five

Plots for the Small to Medium Age Group

> A novel is a mirror walking along the main road.
>
> Stendhal

What is a story? It is a form of authority. If I tell you a story, you are almost certain to listen. A story is easier to follow, and therefore to remember, than a chain of disconnected facts, because it has causality, one event leads to another. It is like swimming with the current — whereas memorising unrelated facts is like swimming upstream.

E. M. Forster damned the story (alas) in *Aspects of the Novel;* he made fun of Neanderthal Man, listening to the tribal storyteller, kept awake only by suspense.

> What would happen next? The novelist droned on, and as soon as the audience guessed what happened next, they either fell asleep or killed him . . .
>
> E. M. Forster, *Aspects of the Novel*

But what E.M.F. refers to so disparagingly as a story is, in fact, not a story at all, but a mere narrative. His definition of *plot* is what *I* would call a story: 'The king died, and then the queen died of grief.'

The difference between life and a story is that life is flat and goes on and on, whereas a story has a shape, which resists alteration; take out one piece and it pulls the whole structure lopsided; it has a frame, a climax; you listen in confidence because you know that *something is going to happen,* it will all work out in the end. So the writer must ensure that something *does* happen.

Something must certainly happen in a children's story, and it must happen in a causal, connected way; not in answer to the question *what happened next,* but in answer to the question, *why?*

Very small children, of course, are happy enough with saga plots, such as Old Mother Hubbard (a masterpiece of inconsequentiality); but they are even more delighted if a story visibly winds up and then unwinds again:

> She went a little farther and she met a cat:
> Cat, cat, kill rat,
> Rat won't gnaw rope,
> Rope won't beat dog,
> Dog won't bite pig etc . . .
>
> *Then:* the cat began to kill the rat,
> The rat began to gnaw the rope,
> The rope began to beat the dog.
> The dog began to bite the pig,
> Piggy jumped over the stile,
> And the old woman got home that night.

The Old Woman who Bought a Pig is a model of causality.

Many folk and fairy tales have a retributive pattern: a situation is set up with A always unkind to B; then B successfully undergoes some kind of trial, quest, or ordeal, and is rewarded; A, jealous, insists on also having a go at the ordeal, and due to faults in A's nature, fails miserably and is punished. Grimm is full of tales built on this pattern, the pretty sister and the ugly sister. Small to medium age children love them because, as soon as they are acquainted with the basic pattern, the end is in view from the start, and so is all the more enjoyable. They can tell that A will fail, and look forward to each failure.

As children grow more sophisticated, and accustomed to the pattern of folk tales, they begin to enjoy stories that may start from the traditional pattern and then diverge, either making fun of the original form or using it as a basis for new invention.

Saki made use of this idea in his short story *The Story Teller,* where children respond joyfully to a tale in which the good little girl is eaten up by the wolf just *because* she was so very good — she was the only one allowed to walk in the park, and the wolf's attention was attracted by the sound of her medals clanking. Children — once past the nursery age — develop a subversive streak (they have to, to survive, since they live under continual subjection); so a subversive element in their fiction has a strong appeal to them, and makes a safe outlet for their rebellious feelings.

How do you get your ideas?

> Nothing is more dangerous than an idea, when it is the only idea we have.
>
> Alain, *Libres-propos*

How do you get your ideas?

This is the question relating to plots that is most frequently addressed by amateurs to professional writers; and the professionals are always amazed that the acquisition of ideas can ever seem a problem, since to them ideas seem plentiful as blackberries in September.

It is a question of approach.

If you are a cook, you would not expect to be able to produce a meal from an empty kitchen. Each time you go out, your marketing eye is alert for useful ingredients; and when you enter your kitchen, it already contains all the staples, and plenty of useful tidbits which will suggest dishes in themselves.

In the same way, a working writer is always on the alert. Even the short walk to the post office may contain material for fiction: the little man, thinking he is unobserved, nipping with great agility through the narrow gap between a lamp post and a street sign, just for fun; a cat up on a high ledge; an odd reflection in a shop window, making it seem as if a swan is sitting on a cafeteria counter; something thrown out of a bus window that looks like an egg . . . ; a man who breaks a bottle of milk in the dairy.

Then there are overheard conversations, always a fruitful source of conjecture: somebody in a voice of outrage exclaiming, 'And he *did* it! In front of her! And she was his own *wife*!' Or: 'He went on wheeling her about in that chair for *nine years*!' Or: 'The girl had just tipped Father's ashes into her dustpan.' Or: 'When he got home, there was a note from his wife that said, "Spider got out. I am at Aunt Ethel's."'

Quite the most teasing bit of talk I ever heard was between two men in the London underground. 'Did I ever tell you the story of the mushroom?' said A. He had the voice of a real raconteur, rich and assured. 'No, what happened?' said B. 'Well, there were only two officers in charge. And they'd had the parade ground Hoovered. Lord, these Germans are thorough! You could have rolled out pastry on that parade ground.' 'What about the mushroom?' 'I was coming to that. There was this white flagpole, you see, in the middle of the parade ground —' At this point the train came to Charing Cross and they got out. I have always had it in mind to write the story of the mushroom, but haven't got round to it yet. Meanwhile it is open to all. In any case, every use made of it would be different.

Newspaper items are another excellent source of material:

The wretched couple who buy a bungalow only to find that it has a public right-of-way through its garden — and the wife is ill . . . The man prosecuted for keeping his show stallion in a shed, never letting it out; the girl who falls off her bike and is taken to hospital where the hospital authorities quite unjustly suspect parental battering and won't release her; the bulb grower who needs someone else to house his whole field of tulips for a year; the security firm sued because a guard dog won't bite a naked person; the cobra set to guard a royal sapphire; the gipsy who put a curse on the town council, or the religious sect who put a curse on archaeologists excavating a tomb (yes, I know; a corny old line, but there was actually a news story about it in the *Guardian*, two days before I wrote this.)

Also in newspapers are small ads. and they are equally productive: 'Balloon (Around the World type) capable of carrying two men plus small cargo required . . .' 'Eccentric but reliable ex-lawyer would like to join expedition to Central America . . .' 'Four landlubbers planning sail round world seek crew . . .' 'Writer wishes rent genuine haunted house, guarantees not to disturb ghost . . .' 'Model Rhinoceros wanted . . .' 'Agile bagpiper with waterproof kilt required . . .' 'Will any Baron not requiring his robes next Tuesday . . .' 'Circular staircase, iron, 10 ft 6 by 3 ft 9, seen erected Hampstead . . .' 'Entries for national snake-charming competition in South Kensington . . .' 'Wanted, bearded man prepared to keep shaving and re-growing beard . . .' 'Would exchange gentleman's library for Jersey herd . . .' (These were all genuine *Times* advertisements.)

Notices seen in the street often produce ideas. 'Fried carpet,' says a huge sign near Kennedy Airport. 'Worm wheels, bevels, helicals, and spur gears,' reads a notice in a shop window. 'Rapid service for own blanks.' Once I smashed my glasses and had to grope about without them, purblind, for two weeks; the notices I misread during that time gave me material for several stories.

Then there are the startling things that happen to your friends and acquaintances: someone's car becoming hooked on to the back of a truck full of tombstones; a woman who discovers that her two-year-old twins, when dressed alike, cannot see one another; a woman, who, when she is pregnant, has premonitions of events that later come to pass; a child who hates his school lunch so much that he puts it into his gumboots.

Once you have begun collecting ideas you see them everywhere. Not, of course, necessarily such zany ones as the examples I have chosen; you collect the ideas that suit *you*.

There are the things which are so familiar that you may have accepted them for years until you begin looking for story-themes: an old neighbour's habit of summoning his cat to dinner by banging on a tin plate . . . An object in the local museum which may only be touched by a descendant of the donor . . . A house stacked high with overdue library books . . .

Our whole surroundings are composed of basic material for plots, once the habit of *recognising* them has been acquired.

Dreams can also be a fertile source.

> 'L — d!' said my mother. 'What is all this story about?'
> Laurence Sterne, *Tristram Shandy*

Very soon, you will have found that selecting the germinal idea is no problem. But then what? One idea on its own is not enough.

You need a theme to give it direction.

Themes

Themes, on the whole, are basic and simple.

If you consult a textbook on creative writing, the plot chapter is likely to present you with a framework consisting of something like this: a character's intention — an obstacle — attempts to overcome obstacle — preliminary failure — ultimate success. What could be more quenching? I would find it almost imposible to launch a plot off a single character and his intention — whereas it is the easiest thing in the world to begin from a *situation*.

Some opening situations, for instance, are surefire winners: a deathbed promise (Wilkie Collins was an expert at this); a horrible piece of injustice; somebody in disguise, like Ivanhoe, which instantly evokes the question, *why* is he in disguise, what has been happening to him?

Many situations almost automatically set up fictional possibilities: Neighbour A asks Neighbour B to pull down a bit of his garden wall so that A can get a view from his kitchen window. B refuses.

A ten-year-old girl goes round filling up a notebook with answers to a self-invented questionnaire on adults' habits.

A friend's character is disastrously altered by a car crash.

Another friend, a gout patient, always carries colchicine, which is a poison.

An old lady believes that she will die if her son ever digs up his asparagus bed.

A vain father won't let his twenty-year-old daughter wear glasses.

While choosing themes for children's stories, it is often useful to take another look at basic myth and folktale plots. An archetypal one is that of the son setting out on a quest for his lost father, as in the stories of Theseus, Cuchulain, Oedipus, Jason, Siegfried and Buster Keaton. Can this be transferred to a contemporary setting? Yes, obviously it can, for Buster Keaton did it. What variations could there be? Does the son find his father? Or not? Perhaps he only *imagined* that his father was lost?

The picaresque story, which may arise from the quest theme,

simply occupies the whole book in getting the character from A to B. This, if you have fertility of invention, can be very successful. A classic example is Sheila Burnford's *The Incredible Journey.* An earlier (and equally gripping one) is *The Pilgrim's Progress.*

Arising from the father-quest we find the theme of the hero who is at odds with his world, or lives in a world of his own. Shakespeare makes considerable use of this — in Hamlet, Twelfth Night, The Taming of the Shrew, Timon, Lear . . . So did Cervantes in Don Quixote. Sometimes this theme can lead to comedy — more often, to tragedy.

> A story has been thought to its conclusion when it has taken its worst possible turn.
> Friedrich Durrenmatt, *The Physicists*

It gives you a good launch-off point if your novel begins in the very middle of a really bad situation: a country in a state of tyranny; a family in dire straits of poverty; invasion of the goodies by detestable interlopers; the loss — by death, illness, imprisonment, journey — of some loved, important character.

Or, conversely, you can begin your novel in a situation of idyllic affluence and happiness, a kind of Golden Age, give just a glimpse of it, and *then* have your characters abruptly jolted out of it into the grimness of reality; Hodgson Burnett did this in *A Little Princess,* George MacDonald did it in *The Princess and Curdie,* Nesbit did it in *The Treasure Seekers* (indeed it is a theme of many of her books), J. M. Barrie did it in his play *The Admirable Crichton* (which also employs the reversal, tables-turned motif which can be an ingredient of humour). Now the theme of your book, ready-made, is the main character's struggle to return to the lost state — or, ultimately, his acceptance of life as it is.

Revenge is a prevailing theme of folk tales; in fact Norse, Icelandic, and Teutonic sagas seem to consist of almost nothing *but* revenge. Rudyard Kipling's stories are laced with revenge. Mowgli kills Shere Khan, and lets in the jungle on the village that turned him out. And, of course, children greatly enjoy such stories; children are still primitive enough to be delighted when the villains are ground in the dust and humiliated.

But we, twentieth century adults, have studied psychology and know that revenge *is* primitive; a longing for vengeance is merely a hatred of the devil we are subconsciously aware of in ourselves; so perhaps we ought not to offer it to young readers? This decision must remain with the individual. Perhaps we can make use of the revenge motif as O. Henry did in his story *The Moment of Victory;* show that such motivation can lead to an immense amount of wasted time and anticlimax; or, as Saki did in his story *The Interlopers,* that the feud of the two main characters can be reduced to absurdity by outside circumstances (Shakespeare did it, too, in *Romeo and Juliet*). Children are intensely interested in morality, and if you can actually display, episode by episode, the corrosive effect of something like a revenge impulse on a personality, they will be with you every step of the way.

The redemption of an unpleasant character is a theme that appeals strongly to children. *The Secret Garden* is all about the reclamation of the bad-tempered Mary and the hypochondriac Colin. *Captains Courageous* transforms precocious, sickly Harvey into a normal boy. *The Chaplet of Pearls* develops spoilt little Eustacie into a heroine. (The nineteenth century was very addicted to the redemption theme; but it is still a good one.) A variation of this theme, of course, is the apparently helpless, ineffective hero rolling up his sleeves and reforming his unpromising surroundings. The classic example of this, on an adult level, is Nevil Shute's *A Town Like Alice,* in which the heroine transforms the miserable desert settlement into a place where she can happily spend the rest of her life. Charlotte Yonge does the same thing in *The Dove in the Eagle's Nest,* where gentle little Christina sets to and reforms a castle full of brigands. And it has also been done by Stella Gibbons in *Cold Comfort Farm!*

Building the reader's interest

> There is pleasure in hardship heard about.
>
> Euripides

Having your basic idea — or, preferably, several ideas, you can't have too many — and your theme, and your opening situation — how do you go about building and maintaining the reader's interest?

Children won't stand for being bored. A child reader is like a wary and agile fish — to keep his attention you have to bait your hook with cunning and play him with all the angler's art, you have to keep the action continuously moving. Furthermore (to mix the metaphor) you have to strew little intriguing clues and nuggets of information along the way, so as to keep his interest from flagging.

There are various ways of doing this.

One, when you have engaged plenty of interest and sympathy in your main character, is to make him suffer fearful hardships. Then the sympathetic reader will *have* to go on reading, if only to find out whether matters improve.

It is all too easy to lose interest in a character who is in a comfortable, happy situation.

Another means of heightening the reader's interest is to issue some warning.

'There is a traitor among us,' Character A advises Character B, 'but I don't know who it is.' That immediately makes your reader look sharply around for the possible villain; maybe he will be able to spot the fiend before the hero does.

An element of mystery is always valuable — something glimpsed, overheard, not fully understood, remembered; a hint dropped, a prophecy, an oracle, something to puzzle both hero and reader, to make them feel that there is more, here, than meets the eye. John Masefield did this beautifully in his two children's books, *The Midnight Folk* and *The Box of Delights;* they are full of strange, significant references, half of which *are never explained.* And does this matter? Of course not! Because enough *is* explained so that what is left enigmatic seems to be just, tantalisingly, out of reach.

Make sure that, wherever the action is taking place, you yourself have the scene in which it is happening *completely visualised* in your mind's eye. It should be as clear to you as a photograph, as a film sequence. If you, the writer, can't see it clearly, how can the reader possibly be expected to do so?

Beginning

At such a time I found out for certain that this bleak place overgrown with nettles was the churchyard . . . and that the dark, flat wilderness beyond the churchyard, intersected with dykes and mounds and gates, with scattered cattle feeding on it, was the marshes . . .

'Hold your noise!' cried a terrible voice, as a man started up from among the graves at the side of the church porch. 'Keep still, you little devil, or I'll cut your throat!' A fearful man, all in coarse grey, with a great iron on his leg. A man with no hat, and with broken shoes, and with an old rag tied round his head. A man who had been soaked in water, and smothered in mud, and lamed by stones, and cut by flints, and stung by nettles, and torn by briars, who limped and shivered and glared and growled . . .

Charles Dickens, *Great Expectations*

Could you have a better opening than that? On page 1, the bleak scene and the terrifying convict are already set before you.

It is impossible to be too speedy with the beginning of a children's book. You have to rush the reader off his feet, if possible, with the first paragraph. Moreover, children are full of conservatism and prejudice, so you may be battling against unknown odds.

It took me years to begin *Little Women* because I was so put off by some grumbling character called Jo who appeared in the first line; I thought the name Jo, without an e, horribly low and vulgar, and if he was going to *grumble* all the time as well . . .! Disgustedly, when I was six or seven, I kept peering at the book and putting it back on the shelf; not till the age of eight did I discover that Jo was a girl, and begin to fall in love with the March family.

If you can toss your hero into an exciting predicament right at the start, then, by seeing him through it, the reader will have time to get used to him.

Tom Sawyer opens with Aunt Polly chasing Tom, who has been stealing jam; Peter Dickinson starts *The Weathermonger* with two children marooned on a tiny islet on Weymouth Bay while the entire population of Weymouth wait eagerly for them to be drowned by the tide.

All the basic information as to who these characters are must wait to be administered in small doses later on; a children's writer can't afford to start at a leisurely pace like Scott:

In that pleasant district of merry England which is watered by the river Don, there extended in ancient times a large forest covering the greater part of the beautiful hills and valleys which lie between Sheffield and the pleasant town of Doncaster . . .

(*Ivanhoe*)

Such a sentence makes you hear the sound of books slapping shut all over the library.

If you can startle your readers with your opening, do that too. One of my favourite stories when I worked on the magazine began with the words: 'The most memorable day of my life was the one when my father hit me with a haddock . . .'

Any editor would be predisposed in favour of *that* story!

Keeping them interested

> Creation sleeps. 'Tis as the general pulse
> Of life stood still, and Nature made a pause;
> An awful pause!
>
> Edward Young, *Night thoughts*

Sometimes your story seems to come to a halt. This is known as Writer's Block. There is nothing much you can do about it. You have to allow time for natural processes. You just have to wait, every now and then taking a look to see if anything is happening. Sometimes you are waiting for a new, necessary idea to float up from the depths of your mind and lock the whole thing together.

Sometimes the idea seems to be magically provided from outside. A street sign gives you the idea for your title. You step over a grating and notice, down below, a key that somebody has dropped. The shop has a sign up saying Closed, due to Death in Family.

You see an old man, well dressed but hatless, sitting on a bench in pouring rain, gazing intently, tragically, into his loaded shopping bag.

These may seem like random occurrences, *but you would not have noticed them* if they had not been relevant to what is going on inside. Your mind is selecting all the time.

> The villain still pursued her.
>
> Milton Nobles

Your block has unblocked, and you are off again.

What other means are there of accelerating the pace?

You can have a time factor. The heroine is going to be executed by such-and-such a date (as in *The Heart of Midlothian*); the Queen's diamonds have to be recovered before the King realises that she has given two of them to her lover (as in *The Three*

Musketeers); the wife's head is going to be chopped off at daybreak (as in *Bluebeard*).

Old methods are often the best.

You can also accelerate the pace of the action, or seem to, by having it happen to the accompaniment of dialogue:

> 'Oh, my God! He's fallen under the train!'
> 'Wave a flag at the driver! *Run,* you fool!' etc etc.

The reader's imagination will then do half the work for you, and you get the effect of several things happening at once (as indeed they do in real life).

An enclosed world makes an excellent setting for a children's novel — school, island, prison, workhouse, occupied territory; or, the world may be surrounded, not by physical barriers but by moral ones. Family subjugation can achieve this, or straight threat: the barriers are really set up by the central character's fear of reprisals if he tries to appeal to the outside world for help. Chesterton achieves this in *The Man Who Was Thursday,* Wilkie Collins in *The Woman in White*. The heroes and their friends are totally encompassed by the villains, who seem to be omnipresent, omniscient. Cries for help go unheard or (another heightener of tension) are intercepted, making matters worse.

> [Uncle Silas] rose like a spectre with a white scowl. 'Then how do you account for that?' he shrieked, smiting my open letter, face upward, upon the table.
>
> J. Sheridan le Fanu, *Uncle Silas*

Such a denouement between hero and villain (who, up to this moment, has been pretending that he is *not* a villain) always comes as a shattering shock. Be sure that you do not make use of it too early in the book.

Ending

> Great is the art of beginning, but greater the art is of ending.
>
> Longfellow, *Elegiac Verse*

If beginnings are important, endings are *crucially* important. In fact it is an excellent plan to have a firm and clear picture of the end in your mind before you ever begin to write; even, perhaps, have the last paragraph written down.

Children often wish to deny the end of a story if they can. They feel bereaved, or even frightened, by the thought that a favourite story has come to a stop. A story to them is like a friend, a live entity. My daughter once wrote to C. S. Lewis, whose Narnia books she adored, asking what happened after the last one, how the story *really* ended. She was very troubled when he wrote back saying that he didn't know the end, because it hadn't happened yet. To children the end of a story represents chaos and uncertainty, being faced with emptiness, with something insoluble, with death itself.

Naturally this fear gives rise to the repetitive type of inter-linked folk saga, where one tale leads to endless others; and, in our own folk culture, to soap opera and books with hundreds of sequels; doubtless due to children writing and begging for 'one more book about Pollyanna — or Anne of Green Gables — or Tarzan — or Mary Poppins.'

So how can a children's writer deal with this problem of the dangerous end?

A flat or unsatisfactory ending is the worst sin a writer can commit; it renders the whole book null and void. So the end, when it comes, must be strong, satisfying, yet perhaps with an element of surprise in it, so that the reader may feel, 'Yes, I see; yes, of course. Yes, it *had* to happen that way.'

The texture of a story makes a whole lot of difference to the way the final conclusion is going to affect the reader. If there are real, live characters, and good strong relationships; if the story has resonance, so that echoes seem to go off from it into real life all around; if it has a lot of vivid detail supporting and enriching it, so that there is more substance than the mere mechanics of plot; if there are meanings and actions not fully explained, connections and richnesses interwoven simply for the interest and pleasure of the writer (and therefore of the reader as well) — then the end, when it comes, will not be merely a flat dismissal, but will be a rounding-off; the reader will want to go back and reflect and ponder on what has been happening; in a way, the story never *will* be over, because it will go on working in his mind. You have only to look at the works of great writers to see the validity of this. A story by Chekhov, even the very simplest, like the heartbreaking one about the little boy who wants to write a letter to his grandfather but doesn't know the address — a story like that seems to have no beginning or end, *it is happening all the time.*

Should the end be happy or sad?

Happy, I believe. Children up to the age of thirteen or fourteen are not ready for tragic endings, and certainly not for gloomy or ambiguous ones. In folk or fairy tales, right is bound to triumph, and children in the middle age bracket are still not wholly separated from the fairy tale world; they will soon come to see that the victory of reason and virtue at the end of a story is an assertion of principle rather than a statement of fact; but they have not yet reached the stage when they wish to face, or should be required to, the worst potential of reality.

So it is not a bad idea to cheer the end of your book with a bit of light relief. If your climax has achieved the depth and resonance that will leave the readers moved, pierced, thoughtful — then let them down gently in a postscript, perhaps by bringing back some minor character and allowing him to perform his act for a moment or two, whatever it is — losing his spectacles *again,* asking the time, setting the table for tea — just to close the door gently, not with a violent bang.

This gives a feeling of completion, of tidying up your enclosed world.

Exercise

When you are thinking about plots, set your mind consciously to work. Consider the scenes in fiction that have impressed/frightened/entertained/touched you most. Consider their mechanics.

Was it because there was an 'if only' element?

If only Cordelia hadn't lost her temper, if only the Indian gentleman had known that Sara Crewe was just the other side of the wall, if only Jo had gone, instead of delicate little Beth, to visit the sick family . . .

Chapter Six

Character

> When characters are really alive, before their author, the
> latter does nothing but follow them in their action.
>
> Luigi Pirandello,
> *Six Characters in Search of an Author*

Beginners often suffer from a form of mental block when they first
tackle the problem of character construction — especially main
characters; minor ones are easier, because they can be made two-
dimensional. But heroes and heroines can seem appallingly blank.

'How can I create a person out of thin air?' the beginner asks
fearfully, as if some Nostradamus-type witchcraft were going to be
demanded. Or, looking round at friends, relations, and colleagues,
so inconsistent, many-sided, complicated, familiar, and at the same
time teasingly hard to depict: 'How could I ever possibly describe
him? Or *her*? It would be like trying to make a pencil sketch of
Westminster Abbey.'

It is true that if you try to make a portrait of a person you know
very well, you are burdened with too much information. You
hardly know where to start. Which is a good reason for not using
real people in your fiction; another is the possibility of libel
actions.

How are characters created?

How can a writer grapple with these difficulties: on the one hand,
the construction of a character from nothing at all; on the other, a

selection from an unwieldy amount of detail.

How do you begin to build up character? How do you fit your characters into the plot? Writers are often asked this, as if characters were raisins in a cake mix.

In reality the process is reversed. The plot grows from the characters; or plot and characters grow together.

Let us suppose a plot consisting of a feud between two neighbours. Character A, a successful lawyer, has swindled Character B, a poor farmer, out of a valuable bit of land, and now hopes to get control of his pleasant little farm as well. Their two children, young Miss C and Master D, are fond of each other, and would like to be friends, but the family situation won't allow it. However C, with her metal detector, has found a buried Roman villa on the land that A is after. A doesn't know about this and D swears C to secrecy, but she has already told her mother, Mrs A . . .

For basic motivations in a plot such as this, it can be a useful stimulant to cast through the seven deadly sins: pride, covetousness, lust, anger, gluttony, envy, sloth; it is easily seen in our skeleton that Character A is motivated by envy and covetousness, Character B by anger and pride.

Here, in fact, is a plot directly based on human emotions. A, the lawyer, has to be jealous, grasping, unscrupulous; B, the farmer, combative, fatally ready to take offence and begin a fight. Perhaps it was his attitude in the first place that set A on his path of acquisitive hostility. And A has guilt in his mind towards B which makes him all the more ready for battle. Mrs A is weak (greedy, perhaps?), reasonably well-meaning, but dominated by her husband; her daughter C is a nice little thing, warm-hearted, unaware of these undercurrents; young D is a fighter like his father, but better educated, with more humour . . .

You see how already your characters begin to tug at their ropes and take shape in the wind. Now is the time to explore them further, to think carefully about each one. As soon as you have their basic motivation established, secondary features and qualities will soon declare themselves. You have to think really hard about these people: what kind of clothes they wear, food they eat, books they read — their dreams, ailments, inner thoughts, daily habits must all be familiar to you. All this information will not be given to the reader — indeed hardly one per cent of it will — but *you* must know it.

Unpleasant characters are much easier to portray than attractive ones. How can one create a convincing good character? Even Dickens fell down here; his Cheerybles, Fenwigs and Brownlows are among his least satisfactory creations.

For a start, it is a great mistake to make a good character *too* good, particularly if he is your hero. A hero or heroine who is perfect all through can be nothing but a dead bore and offers no possibility of development (since, in a children's book, it is undesirable for the main character to deteriorate and go to the bad. It was done in *Eric or Little by Little,* but who reads *Eric* now?)

Much better begin with a faulty central character, who by degrees learns a few things, and grows up in the course of the story.

Consider *The Tailor of Gloucester.* The whole charm of that book lies, not in the ailing old tailor nor in the goody-goody little mice, but in the rather ambivalent character of Simpkin the cat, who begins by flatly disobeying his master and neglecting him, imprisons mice under teacups, but then, later, moved to contrition by their neighbourly behaviour in sewing the waistcoat, amends his ways, takes the tailor a cup of tea, and learns to maintain an entente with mice.

(Reconciliation of enemies is an excellent theme: one that cannot be engaged without careful character delineation.)

Remember that the reader has to feel some emotion towards your characters — empathy, affection, exasperation, or curiosity — he has to be interested enough to care what happens next and want to go on reading about these people.

Extending your characters

When you have some half-formed characters floating around like tadpoles in a fermenting plot, a useful way of encouraging their growth is to check through single attributes which have excited your interest, devotion, or irritation in friends and acquaintances, and try if some variant of these will help to fill in an outline. Never describe a whole person — select one attribute.

You know a person who always smiles a little before saying something that is going to hurt or annoy the hearer. Take this habit on its own and fit it on to your Character A: at once he becomes more solid. A thin, middle-aged man . . . you begin to imagine his dry, chalky skin, which wrinkles when he moves his head, the triumphant look in his eye, the way he says, smiling, 'Of course it's none of *my* business, but . . .'

Depicting your characters

> Everyone is . . . a very great, very important character!
> Ugo Betti, *The Burnt Flower Bed*

Characters can be depicted in three ways.

(1) The first is by flat description. But, as I stated in Chapter One, the writer of a children's book must ration himself to very, very little flat description indeed. In any case flat description is rather crude and cumbrous.

(2) Better by far try the second method, displaying your character's nature and habits through the medium of dialogue:

> 'You were flirting with her during the whole night,' said Madame Mantalini. 'I had my eye upon you all the time.'
> 'Bless the little winking twinkling eye; was it on me all the time!' cried Mantalini in a sort of lazy rapture. 'Oh demmit!'
> Charles Dickens, *Nicholas Nickleby*

The reader can learn practically all there is to know about the Mantalinis in these four lines — that the wife is sour, practical, jealous, the husband an irresponsible teasing ogler. Dickens reduced the speech identification of his minor characters to an art: Micawber, Mantalini, Gamp, Weller, Miggs — they all announce themselves like so many radio stations.

Particularly in a children's book, it is useful if a character has such a distinctive way of speaking that he can be instantly recognised. It saves putting in 'he said' and 'she replied' all the time, and is a great help if the book is read aloud — and one assumes that a large proportion of children's books will be read aloud.

(3) The third way of demonstrating your character is, of course, by a piece of action.

In *Kidnapped*, Robert Louis Stevenson has the hero, David Balfour, visit his unknown uncle. At breakfast Uncle Ebenezer, already established as a 'mean, narrow-shouldered clay-faced creature', pauses before drinking his ale to ask if David wants some too.

57

I told him such was my habit, but not to put himself about.

'Na, na,' said he, 'I'll deny you nothing in reason.'

He fetched another cup from the shelf; and then, to my great surprise, instead of drawing more beer, he poured an accurate half from one cup to the other. There was a kind of nobleness in this that took my breath away; if my uncle was certainly a miser, he was one of that thorough breed that goes near to make tne vice respectable.

Robert Louis Stevenson, Kidnapped

That little touch with the beer saves paragraphs of dissertation on Uncle Ebenezer's parsimony. One can imagine Stevenson joyfully observing such a piece of meanness somewhere and storing it in his mind for future use.

So note down all such episodes that might enrich and enliven your characters: the annoying repetitive use of a word or phrase, the woman who always says, 'It's a moot point,' when she intends to have her own way; the boy who takes an immensely long time to make up his mind over every trifle; the girl who instantly falls ill if any demand is ever made on her; the fussy elder who is always ready with a reminder *before* it is necessary; the person who feels impelled to contradict any statement as soon as it is made; the woman who says 'we' not 'I' automatically including her husband and children in any statement; the acquaintance who always takes care to let you know what a lot they do for their friends, the one who puts you in the wrong by exaggerating their own suffering; the glutton who glances round at meals to see how others have fared; the sponger who blithely accepts hospitality and does nothing in return; the touchy pride that takes offence at offers of help; the namedropper who refers to 'my friend Lady Elsinor,' or 'as Larry Oliver was saying to me'; the obsessional hoarder who has boxes full of smoothed-out chocolate wrappers; the inventive liar whose fabrications continually put him in difficulties; the boy who detests discipline to such a degree that if told to do anything he does the exact opposite; the girl who longs for a brother so much that she invents an imaginary one and actually goes to meet him off the train . . .

Children relish distinctive, well-drawn characters.

But can the characters of children be drawn as sharply as those of adults, with an equal degree of light and shade?

Certainly they can.

Obviously no child character would have had time, in its short life, to develop the degree of miserliness depicted by Stevenson in Uncle Ebenezer; but even very small children may show remarkably firm and original traits and behaviour patterns. Think of the youngest brother, Donald, in Enid Bagnold's *National Velvet,* who collects spit in a bottle and dominates his elder sisters. Or passionate little Polly Home, who appears as a tiny child in the first chapter of Charlotte Bronte's *Villette,* and then is not seen again until two thirds of the way through the book; but her character has been so well established that she is immediately recognisable again when she appears, grown up, as Paulina Mary.

In the twenties and thirties, character tended to be neglected, if not omitted altogether, in children's fiction; children were usually depicted in groups, undergoing communal adventures, as if they had not the capacity to be individuals, and half-a-dozen children were roughly the equivalent of one adult; it was not until the forties that robust development of character began again to be observable in the work of such authors as T. H. White, who could write:

Gawaine was passionate; Agravaine was sulky; Gaheris was stupid; and Gareth was a dear . . . Gawaine was not exactly bright but at least he was sturdy, loyal, and warmhearted. His only fault was that he could not control his temper . . . Agravaine was the bully; but he was cowardly, and horribly jealous for his mother.

T. H. White, *The Witch in the Wood*

A character can only show his nature in relations with other people; he can't function in a vacuum. Often the hero's relationship with a minor character turns out to be an important and pivotal part of the story. Don Quixote could hardly get on without Sancho Panza, or Don Giovanni without Leporello. Huck's relationship with Jim runs like a spinal cord through *Huckleberry Finn.* David Balfour's friendship with Alan Breck, and growing love for Catriona, are far more engaging and memorable than the rather muddled adventures that he undergoes in Stevenson's *Kidnapped* and *Catriona.* Indeed Alan and Catriona, both beautifully depicted, spirited, faulty characters, are more interesting than David himself. Frequently a minor character can steal the limelight from the hero; sometimes even an animal does this, as the ugly, lovable dog Lina, in *The Princess and Curdie,* or the Parrot Polynesia in the Dolittle books.

Writers often find that characters grow on their own, subconsciously constructed and embellished from uncounted scraps and hints. Which is another reason why a writer must be constantly observant.

Villains

Villains can be even more important than heroes. A story *can* just scrape along with a cardboard hero; many of Buchan's and Rider Haggard's books do; and what do we really know of Robin Hood, Perseus, or King Arthur, save their handiness at rescuing damsels in distress? But your villain is no use at all unless he poses a real threat, and has the power to put the reader in a fright.

How do you achieve this?

First, he must arrive early enough in the book. And the reader must be well aware of his power. A demonstration of this on a minor character may give the desired effect.

The wicked queen Catherine de Medici, in Dumas' *Marguerite de Valois,* murders a poor messenger by arranging for him to fall through a trap into an oubliette, and then descends a thousand steps to remove a letter from the dead body; this at once gives the reader an idea of the lengths that Catherine is prepared to go to in order to have her way. From that moment, Catherine and the oubliette are at the back of the reader's mind.

If, early on, you show your gangster boss upending a rival in a tub of liquid concrete, the reader knows what may be in store for the hero. (And if the hero does *not* know, that makes it all the more menacing.)

Stevenson, a master hand at creating fear situations, made use of an infallible ingredient in *Treasure Island* — villains with physical disabilities: Blind Pew, whose entry into the book is a most terrifying scene, and Long John Silver, one of the best villains in fiction. Why should a villain with a wooden leg be more frightening than one with all his faculties intact? We perhaps feel, superstitiously and illogically, that a handicapped person may have developed supernormal powers, may feel supernormal malice and vindictiveness.

Whatever the reason, handicapped villains have held the stage from classic times: the one-eyed Cyclops, lame Vulcan, Richard Crookback, one-handed Captain Hook, one-legged Long John, the albino villain of Jamaica Inn. In one of Stevenson's most hair-raising scenes, two boys are pursued by a blind leper; the combination is almost *too* bloodcurdling.

Conan Doyle makes Sherlock Holmes's enemy, the arch-criminal Moriarty, sinister by hardly ever showing him; only when some particularly fiendish crime has been committed, Holmes shakes his head and says 'Ah, that is Moriarty's work . . .'

> I lost it to a soldier and a foeman,
> A chap that did not kill me, but he tried;
> That took the sabre straight, and took it striking,
> And laughed, and kissed his hand to me, and died.
> A. E. Housman, *I Did Not Lose My Heart*

There can be lovable rogues too.

Rupert of Hentzau, in *The Prisoner of Zenda,* is much better villain-value, because he is more of a rounded character, than the main villain, Prince Michael, who does nothing but snarl. And in *The Hobbit,* the sinister, hissing, but mournful, underground creature Gollum is a thousand times more effective than the dragon Smaug, who is nothing but a dragon.

A smiling villain, with some sympathetic traits, can be ever so much more terrifying than one who is merely hostile; because the reader does not know what he will do next. Sweet silvery-haired Uncle Silas in Sheridan le Fanu's novel; fat agreeable Count Fosco in Wilkie Collins's *The Woman in White* — these have power to chill the blood more than Dracula and all his tribe.

Don't neglect to have plenty of mixed characters — stupid but lovable, bad-tempered but reliable, lovable but wicked, funny but tragic.

You will enjoy creating them, and your readers will enjoy them too.

But should young readers be presented with really hair-raising villains? I believe so. They love to be scared, and are more robust than adults; the brisk sales of horror stories demonstrates that.

Dialogue and dialect

> Speak the speech, I pray you, trippingly . . .
> William Shakespeare, *Hamlet*

Characters, as I said a few paragraphs back, should be readily recognisable by their utterance. Dialogue must be real, individual, and carry the stamp of the speaker.

In order to achieve this, a writer must listen, listen, listen, take mental notes of people's speech patterns, idiosyncrasies, repetitions, hesitancies, misuse of words, the way in which they chuckle, groan, use emphasis, clear their throats, change tone when embarrassed.

While you are writing, make an effort to hear your characters' voices in your mind's ear, to make sure that he, she, and nobody else, could use the words that you are putting into their mouths.

Don't let it be just your own diction.

An exercise for this is to imagine the voice of a well-known friend, relative, your butcher, your boss, your doctor, your bank manager, and imagine how each would utter the same basic message.

Dialect these days in fiction has to be used with great discretion; it must be much more subtle than it was in the nineteenth century, when Cockneys could be allowed to say, 'Yncher goin' ter give us a tanner, Guv?' Farmers talked in broad Mummerset, blacks used the language of Uncle Remus or Uncle Tom, and small children, even in the pages of George Eliot, were made to utter such odious remarks as, 'Munny, my iron's twite told; p'ease put it down to warm . . .'

Fear of snobbery and racism, disgust at sentimentality, dislike of phoniness, and, simply, fashion, have reduced dialect in fiction to a minimum. (Also, books, now competing with film and TV, can't afford to place too many barriers in the reader's way.) So the contemporary writer has to convey dialect, if any, by cadence and word order, rather than by eccentric spelling.

Language in a children's book is crucially important. You are cheek-to-cheek with your reader, you are talking into his ear, you must be *absolutely certain* of your own meanings and intentions, and take the utmost pains to convey them.

There is a virtue, too, in the reader's being aware — even if only subliminally — that the writer is taking these pains, making these efforts, on his behalf. If the efforts include using a few difficult words, then it does no harm for the reader to understand that *he* has to make an effort too, to understand them.

Slang, catch-words, slipshod uses, are therefore wholly out of place in the narrative of a children's book. Characters must speak appropriately, using a slang idiom if that's the way they *would* talk, but avoid in your narrative all such constructions as 'think up' 'meet up', 'plan on', 'contact' used as a verb, and such passing usages as 'with it', 'way out', 'trendy', 'stroppy', 'chuffed', 'browned off', 'bright-eyed and bushy tailed' or any turns of phrase that may happen to be in vogue at the time when you write. Use plain, classic language. In ten years' time you will be glad that you did so; nothing dates a book so horribly as recently out-of-date slang.

This presents a problem for the writer of school stories. Obviously if your characters are school-children they must sound like school-children, and not like Johnson talking to Boswell; but you should take care to flavour their speech with great delicacy, as in using garlic. Much can be done with cadence and word order. William Mayne and Jan Mark have a masterly grasp of school language.

One solution would be to invent your own school slang, which would therefore be dateless.

School stories of past eras seem almost as archaic as Chaucer: '"Calloo, callay, how scrumptiously spiffing!" chortled Raymonde.'

Details

> Don't forget the jewels. They are a detail, but details interest me.
>
> Saki, *Shock Tactics* from *Short Stories of Saki.*

Details are vitally important in children's fiction. They can make the difference between routine run-of-the-mill stuff and Literature with a capital L.

Of course children will read the bald kind of story, one that lacks detail, if it has plenty of action and keeps moving; but that is not the kind of story they go back to fondly again and again. I remember my daughter once picking up a woman's magazine and starting to read a serial in it; the story was laid in the south of France, and the heroine reported, 'We went into the chateau and were served with wine and little cakes.' My daughter flung down the magazine in utter scorn, exclaiming, 'What's the use of that, if she doesn't tell you what *sort* of little cakes?' Ever since then the phrase 'wine and little cakes' has come, in our family, to typify a lazy indifference to detail. And poverty of detail instantly stamps a style as second-rate.

The details are what one chiefly remembers from many books. Think of Elnora's lavish lunchboxes in *A Girl of the Limberlost;* or those little sharp tacks with which the Indian servant fixed bright, strange, foreign embroideries to the wall, in Hodgson Burnett's *A Little Princess:* 'tacks so sharp they could be pressed into the wood and plaster without hammering' — instilling immediate credulity in the reader because if there is one thing any child knows, it is that the sound of hammering will fetch parents at the double.

Remember little Ellen's workbox in *The Wide Wide World:*

> The box was of satinwood, beautifully finished and lined with crimson . . . 'O Mamma, how beautiful . . . Here's a thimble — fits me exactly; and an emery bag — how pretty! and a bodkin — this is a great deal nicer than yours, Mamma, yours is decidedly the worse for wear — and what's this? Oh, to make eyelet holes with, I know. And here are tapes, and buttons, and hooks and eyes, and darning cotton and silk winders and pins . . . Well I shall take great pains now to make my button holes very handsomely.'
>
> Elizabeth Wetherell, *The Wide Wide World*

That passage tells the reader not only about the workbox, but also quite a bit about little Ellen and her Mamma, all in lively dialogue.

Beatrix Potter is excellent on detail.

> Ginger usually requested Pickles to serve them [the mice] because, he said, it made his mouth water. 'I cannot bear,' said he, 'to see them going out at the door carrying their little parcels.'
>
> Beatrix Potter, *The Tale of Ginger and Pickles*

As with the sharp tacks, those little parcels carry instant conviction.

Details are a pleasure to read, and a pleasure to write. If you can pluck out some small common denominator of experience that will instantly register with the reader, you have made yourself a friend.

> It is my bath night and hot milk and 2 wheaty biscuits and 20 minutes read in bed. But the only thing is I have to clean my teeth after biscuits which means getting out again. This hangs over you rather and spoils it.
>
> Sybil Burr, *Life With Lisa*

Exercise

Study your fellow passengers on planes and trains, notice their mannerisms, listen to what they are saying. Think about them inductively, try to imagine the insides of their houses and what they had for breakfast. Try them in your plots. The bus conductor with the long nose, flop of black hair, and sardonic smile — would he do for the hero's friend? The lady making a fuss about smoking in a No Smoking area — would she do for Mrs A? The supercilious bookseller, making it plain he knows far more than his customers — no, he won't fit into this story, but let's keep him for future use, particularly his way of saying, '*So* sorry I can't help' — he might serve as a villain some time.

Chapter Seven

Picture-books

> Sitting safe in nursery nooks
> Reading picture story books.
>
> Robert Louis Stevenson

Unless you are a trained artist, don't try. Certainly don't work your fingers to the bone lovingly preparing a beautiful set of colour illustrations to accompany your text.

I did once hear of a lady who, to illustrate her own small children's story, went to art-school, learned to use the three-colour process, and, after a couple of false starts, brought it off, but it was a long and exhausting business, and she is very much the exception.

Normally you submit the text, and the publisher finds the artist, choosing one they think will complement your work. Some of the artist's previous illustrations will probably be shown you as a sample, you may have the choice of several, and you will have right of veto, and, to some degree, a critical say about the illustrations when produced. That is to say, if you absolutely loathe them, you may state your opinion; but you will not be popular. Illustrators are quite as fidgety as writers about making alterations to finished work, and their work, often, is harder and takes longer. So don't be surprised if your objections are brushed aside.

Do you have any say in the jacket design of a book?

Some. Much depends on the publishers and your relations with them. Some are more amenable than others. On the whole, English publishers are more amenable than American. American publishers' art-departments are so high-powered these days that your complaints will probably fall on deaf ears; you might as well try to alter the Writing on the Wall.

Poetry

> Twice five years
> Or less, I might have been, when first my mind
> With conscious pleasure, opened to the charm
> Of words in tuneful order . . .
>   and for the better part
> Of two delightful hours we strolled along
> Repeating favourite verses with one voice.
>   William Wordsworth, *The Prelude*

Surprisingly, quite a lot of poetry is published for children, and quite a lot of it is terribly bad.

> Every evening, after tea
> Teeny-Weeny comes to me . . .
>   Eugene Field, *Teeny-Weeny* from *Poems of Childhood*

There are, of course, noble exceptions. Ted Hughes, Charles Causley, Roger McGough write poetry that, though it is published as for children, can be admired and appreciated by anybody. C. S. Lewis's criterion for a good child's book was 'a good book which happens, incidentally, to be a book enjoyed by children.' The same is true of poetry.

It is questionable whether poetry should be written specifically for children at all; Messrs Hughes, Causley and McGough, if questioned about it, would almost certainly say they wrote, not for the children, but for themselves.

Anyway, if you do write poetry which seems as if it might be for children, never, never let it be whimsical or coy.

> So come, little child, cuddle closer to me
> In your dainty white nightcap and gown
> And I'll rock you away to that Sugar Plum Tree
> In the garden of Shut-Eye Town.
>   Eugene Field, *The Sugar Plum Tree*

When one surveys some of the books of verse published for children, one can hardly wonder that they put poetry at the bottom of their list. But it is a terrible pity that children in contemporary schools rate poetry so low, when one thinks of all the treasures from the recent and more distant past which they might enjoy.

67

> You may see, if you will look
> Through the windows of this book
> Another child, far far away
> And in another garden, play.
>> Robert Louis Stevenson, *A Child's Garden of Verses*

The current trend is for no rhyme or metre (except in humorous verse and not always then). Each to his own taste, of course, but in a way this seems a waste of children's natural strong attraction to the possibilities of vigorous rhyme and lively rhythm. When they *do* come across a poem such as Alfred Noyes's *The Highwayman,* it knocks them endways.

> Here's a pretty gay book full of verses to sing
> But Lucy can't read it; oh! what a sad thing!
> And such funny stories — such pictures too! — look:
> I am glad I can read such a beautiful book.
>> Jane and Ann Taylor, *Rhymes for the Nursery*

Some excellent volumes of poetry have been published for children during the last fifty years: De la Mare's *Peacock Pie,* Eleanor Farjeon's *Nursery Rhymes of London Town,* Edward Lear's *Book of Nonsense,* Hilaire Belloc's *Cautionary Tales,* T. S. Eliot's *Old Possum's Book of Practical Cats.*

It seems hard to believe that children won't enjoy those, if proffered at the right moment.

In the English language there are innumerable funny poems, galloping poems and tragic, gripping, mysterious poems. If you feel that you can add worthily to these, go ahead; though I should warn you that it is remarkably hard to get a first book of poetry accepted.

The above excerpts from Eugene Field's works are quoted as an example of what to avoid.

Teenage Novels

What is a teenage novel? When was the term first invented? Up until World War II, books were simply divided into adult books and children's books; there was no in-between layer. In 1951 J. D. Salinger, who had begun writing at age fifteen, produced *The Catcher in the Rye,* a moving portrait of an American sixteen-year-old boy having trouble with school and parents. In 1959 *Bonjour Tristesse,* by the eighteen-year-old Françoise Sagan, sold 850,000 copies in France and was widely translated. These two books appeared at the start of what was to be a flood. Then came the Beatles and the whole age of youthful pop. Adolescents suddenly became, not only noticed, but feted, exploited, commercially important. So it has been, ever since. Teenage problems are always good for a newspaper page. The teenage market for clothes, music, electronic equipment, drink, food, magazines, not to mention cigarettes, alcohol, cannabis and amphetamines, now rivals the adult market. Teenagers are more moneyed, mobile and better informed about sex, contraception, drugs, VD, homosexuality and perversion, than they have ever been before.

It is easy to conclude that a great many teenage novels are simply cashing in on this lavish market. If teenagers have the money to buy stereo equipment, jeans with zips in the knees, bright green hair-dos, and trips to Sri Lanka, let them buy a few teenage novels too. Why should they bother to embark on Dostoevsky or the difficulties of Thomas Hardy (both of whom wrote teenage novels, incidentally, if a teenage novel is one that explores the problems of adolescence)? Why not just read *Get Your Ass Out of My Life,* or *Toss Me a Tampon*?

Are teenage novels really necessary? Would it not be better for the fifteen-to-twenty year old age group to apply themselves to *The Awkward Age,* or *War and Peace* or *Romeo and Juliet* (more teenage problems) rather than read the novels of Robert Leeson, Robert Cormier, Paul Zindel, Jan Needle, Judy Blume, all current and skilful practitioners in the teenage field?

That, of course, is an idle question. The teenage novel is here to stay, you can't turn back history. Teenagers who are not yet prepared to grapple with Tolstoy or Henry James do, nevertheless, need something to read. Doubtless it would be more developing for them to read *Jude the Obscure* or contemporary adult writers than some of the books they find on the Young Adult shelves in the library, but, since you can't force books on people, Hardy must wait until they are in the mood.

And, in the meantime, teenage novels discuss their very complicated problems, and can offer an interesting challenge to writers who feel qualified to work in this field.

Qualified?

It is absolutely no use attempting a teenage novel unless (1) you are a teenager yourself and can speak with authority, or (2) you are in constant daily contact with adolescents, either parent, teacher, social worker, or psychiatrist, and consequently familiar with the language, problems, priorities, and complications of being a teenager at the present time.

Trying to grope back to your own teens if they are more than five years removed will not do.

Anybody under twenty regards anybody over twenty-five as having one foot in the grave. And the gap between sixteen and eighteen is immensely greater than that between twenty-six and twenty-eight, or thirty-six and thirty-eight. In fact it is hardly possible to generalise about teenagers, since every month, every week, between the age of thirteen and twenty can bring a profound difference.

> Instead of awakening by the noblest models the FOND and UNMIXED LOVE and ADMIRATION which is the natural and graceful temper of early youth; these nurselings of improved pedagogy are taught to dispute and decide, to suspect all.
> Samuel Taylor Coleridge, *Biographia Literaria*

Teenagers are a marvellous audience if you are equipped to write for them, since they combine lightning quickness and ability to grasp briefly stated ideas (acquired from endless film and TV watching) with unshockability, toughness and a sophisticated sense of humour.

So, in many ways, you are freer in this field than when writing for the medium age group — you need pull no punches, you can give loose rein to satire, if such is your bent, or tragedy, and your readers will be right behind you.

The criteria for teenage novels are, in fact, a complete reversal of those for the medium age group.

No more careful, elaborate plots with well organised happy, or at least optimistic, endings. Teenagers are natural pessimists (and who should blame them?) During this period of their development they are in the process of breaking away from all the rules that have hitherto constrained them. They are not interested in plots; what they *are* interested in is emotion. The teenage novel has a duty to portray the successive tidal waves of feeling that wash over adolescents as they struggle through changing relationships with parents; agonies at school; growing awareness of sex; the search for identity; adjustment to society (or cleavage from it). The teenage novel is a novel of character; in this respect much closer to the adult novel than to novels of the preceding age group.

Subjects? They can be simple, almost minimal. The inevitable drifting apart of siblings; family discord; divorce of parents;

romance, end of romance, and psychological problems are the most common then es.

What to put in, what to leave out?

These are problems that each writer must decide alone. Do you put explicit sex into a teenage novel? This is not a subject on which a guide such as the present work can lay down rules.

However it should here be mentioned that a swing away from permissiveness and towards more censorship is now observable in the USA, where, during 1981, elementary and high-school libraries have become stricter as to which books are considered suitable reading for the young. Fundamentalist groups have been demanding that 'filth be removed from the classroom' and pressure has been put on librarians to withdraw books about sex for children or place them in enclosed areas, subject to parental permission. Several novels by Judy Blume have apparently come under this kind of interdict. The puritan trend has not yet become so pronounced in England (where in any case writing had not yet become so explicit as in the USA) but it seems not unlikely that there will soon be a pendulum swing towards more conventional morality.

Also, before commencing a heady sex novel for sixteen-year-olds, it may be sobering to survey some statistics. In 1946, two hundred fifteen-year-old girls in England and Wales became pregnant each year. By 1978 this number had risen to nearly 5,000 a year. Half the girls who had babies failed to return to school. Birth complications are far more common among teenagers than among adults, haemorrhage and infection more frequent, because of the adolescent girl's physical structure. No form of contraception is suited to the needs of the young. Boys between fourteen and twenty account for over forty per cent of male criminal offences under sentence each year in the UK. Over the past twenty years the crime rate among young males has doubled, that among young females quadrupled. Three out of four teenage marriages break up after two years or less. The age group between fifteen and nineteen is the biggest set of people killed or seriously injured each year on the roads. And during 1981 more heroin came into the UK than ever before.

I do not quote these figures to alarm or shock, merely to make the intending writer pause and consider before writing a story that tends to throw a glamorous light on sex, drugs, or crime.

You have to depict the scene you know; but there are many different ways of doing it. And adolescents, though they seem so hard-headed and canny, are, under their surface maturity, still pathetically easy to influence: witness their wholesale, sheep-like adherence to trends, however bizarre.

So you can't try to justify a glorified portrayal of sex or violence by making your protagonists come to grief at the end of the book. Adolescent readers, even more self-deluding than adults, are quite capable of believing the first half and dismissing the end with 'That wouldn't happen to *me.*'

As it is, teenagers are pressured prematurely into sex and other adult activities by commercial interests and the media; let not the fiction they are offered add to the pressure.

Of course if you want, in your novel, to discuss the effects of this state of affairs and suggest remedies, the field is wide open.

> What a cunning mixture of sentiment, pity, tenderness, irony, surrounds adolescence, what knowing watchfulness!
>
> Georges Bernanos

When writing for adolescents, even more than for younger age groups, it is essential to use straightforward language, not to talk down, above all, not to try to adopt a 'teenage idiom' if it does not come naturally to you. Adolescents are lightning-quick to spot hypocrisy or artificiality.

For some reason, American writers seem able to catch a teenage mode of speech more easily than English ones; perhaps because American speech is already more relaxed, free, and homespun than it is on this side of the Atlantic:

> Meanwhile Eunice is sashaying all over the place wildly thrashing Papa's sword and somehow I've managed to clamber atop the piano. Then Eunice climbs up on the piano-stool and how that rickety contraption survived a monster like her I'll never be the one to tell.
>
> Truman Capote, *My Side of the Matter* from *A Tree of Night*

> They've got the cake mix, the instant frosting, and the pan you bake it in, all inside one box. It's supposed to be so simple there's even a picture on the package of a little girl about six years old whipping the whole thing together. She's so small she's standing on a kitchen chair so she can reach the mixing bowl.
>
> Well, good luck to that little monster on the package. I swear I followed the directions like a paper trail. It looked great when I put it in the oven, but when I took it out it looked like a volcano.
>
> Jim Kirkwood, *There Must be a Pony*

> Used to be you could borrow from your friends, but I don't know, lately it seems to me like all my friends have gone and

married on me. Some of my coolest, finest friends have up and married. I can't get over it. Leaving me right lonesome, and you know how little cash a married man would have free to lend. Seems like they're always saving for an automatic grill and such. There wasn't no hope there.

Anne Tyler, Earthly Possessions

Without resorting to usages such as 'like', 'I mean', 'neat', 'kinda' or 'you know' each of those three paragraphs gives you the exact voice of an adolescent, cautious, ironic, resigned to adverse circumstances.

Suggested reading

If you have not read any teenage novels, before plunging into the genre, you may care to read some of the following: Robert Cormier, *The Chocolate War, I am the Cheese;* Paul Zindel, *My Darling, My Hamburger, The Undertaker's Gone Bananas;* S. E. Hinton, *Tex, The Outsiders;* Robert Leeson, *It's My Life;* Jan Needle, *A Sense of Shame;* Alan Garner, *The Owl Service, Red Shift;* Anne Tyler, *The Tin Can Tree.*

Chapter Eight

Myth and Fantasy

> I wonder if we could contrive some magnificent myth that
> would in itself carry conviction to our whole community.
>
> Plato, *Republic Book 3*

'Fairy tales' as they have come to be loosely designated are about
eighty per cent of them nothing to do with fairies — certainly not
the 'little buzzflies with butterfly wings and gauze petticoats and
shiny stars in their hair, and a wand like a schoolteacher's cane for
punishing bad boys and rewarding good ones,' as Kipling's Puck
scornfully describes fairies in *Puck of Pook's Hill.* Grimm's *Tales,*
if analysed, mostly turn out to be about social problems: over-large
families where the children have, somehow, to be disposed of;
division of property, neighbourly disputes; jealousy among siblings;
marital quarrels. In *Hansel and Gretl* the parents lead the children
into the forest because there is no food; *The Three Brothers* is
about testamentary disposition; *Ashputtel* (Grimm's version of
Cinderella) about sibling hatred. The problems are solved in some
magical manner — which might be called wish-fulfilment — but
the basic structure of the story, in each case, is far from being a
piece of childish whimsy or nonsense; it is a serious social
statement.

That, in fact, is the importance of fairy or folk tales in our
civilisation. The principal ones all deal with basic human problems
which, in one form or another, will always be with us, despite
surface changes in culture. Poverty, jealousy, loss of parents, fear
of the unknown, initiation into adulthood — these are at the root
of children's main anxieties, which are none the less real for being,

mostly, unconscious; and fairy tales, by bringing them out into the open and providing solutions, have an important function, which is, now, well recognised by psychologists and educators.

> Fairy tales, unlike any other form of literature, direct the child to discover his identity and calling.
> Bruno Bettelheim, *The Uses of Enchantment*

Myth is universal experience; fantasy is personal experience.

Children still need myths. In fact, more than ever. Parents are no longer able to replenish and illuminate their children's imaginations by telling them heroic sagas of ancestors, or family ghost stories, or fables that would help link them to the natural world around them. Very likely there is no natural world around them. Most parents can't even — with any truth or sincerity — impart personal accounts of religious or spiritual experiences. Materially our circumstances may have improved; but children in this century seem poorly provided with mental furniture compared — say — with the lavish imaginative equipment of a fifteenth century upbringing; we have no angels, no devils, no dragons, no undiscovered regions of the globe. It is lucky that we at least have space to fall back on; no wonder that science fiction is doing so well. Because, though, of course, children still enjoy stories about giants and witches and dragons, they can't believe in them; it must have been a very different matter when your own parents were afraid of witches, and urged you not to offend the old lady up the road in case she stopped the hens from laying.

A myth or fairy tale, then, interprets and resolves the contradictions which the child sees all around him, and gives him confidence in his power to deal with reality. We don't have angels and devils any more, but we are still stuck with good and evil. A child needs myth to give him a blueprint for behaviour, and to strengthen his imagination. Imagination is a necessary faculty, and modern living gives it little to feed on.

Piaget has said that children are animistic until they reach puberty, that they believe inanimate objects have souls and natures, that the sun shines on us because it loves us and the stone rolls in order to trip us. Personally, I doubt that those beliefs last so long; children nowadays grow up at a frightening speed; poor things, they have the status of maturity thrust on them before they have had much chance to enjoy childhood. As a result, they flounder into a kind of brainwashed adulthood with a feeling that they have been cheated out of whole chunks of childhood, that when they should have been playing Pretend games they were set to reading Situation books. Perhaps pubertal children *are* still animistic but have learned to disguise it by dyeing their hair green and sticking safetypins through their noses. Bettelheim says threateningly in *The Uses of Enchantment:*

> When the unconscious is repressed and its content denied entrance into awareness, then eventually the person's conscious mind will be partially overwhelmed by derivatives of these unconscious elements, or else he is forced to keep such rigid, compulsive control over them that his personality may become severely crippled.

The fact that so many children in their late teens nowadays suffer from periods of depression or disturbance suggests that Bettelheim may be right.

The myth-type story may help to fill this need, by furnishing three basic ingredients: reassurance, emotion, mystery. No doubt this is why fantasy books are so popular among adolescents and those in their early twenties; they replace something that was insufficiently provided in early childhood.

Claude Levi-Strauss has a useful and untranslatable expression, *bricolage;* a *bricoleur* was a kind of odd-job man to the tribe, a gossip, someone who picked up fag-ends of conversation, old left-over images, thoughts, signs, symbols, and shovelled them about into a new pattern. That is what the fantasy writer must hope to achieve.

The term *fantasy* in fiction has been used to cover a fairly wide range of different forms.

I shall divide them into five different categories.

First, fantasy based on traditional myth or legend. This form is both popular and distinguished. T. H. White was one of the innovators, with *The Sword in the Stone* and its sequels, based on the King Arthur legends. Then Tolkien came up with *The Hobbit,* that delightful classic. Both these writers managed to engage humour in their fantasy, which is why, perhaps, these works will stand when others are forgotten; on the whole, humour is an ingredient sadly lacking in fantasy.

Then Tolkien, fascinated by what he had done, produced the Ring trilogy, based loosely, like *The Hobbit,* on Norse mythology. It is grand, heroic, Romantic with a capital R, and has given rise to an amazing and world-wide cult among both adults and children. To my mind it does not have the artistic perfection of *The Hobbit,* but it is certainly worthy of respect. It has also produced a host of imitations, most of them regrettably following its faults rather than its virtues. If you propose to write another of these, you will receive no encouragement from me, but then you will probably not be reading this book.

Other myth-based fantasy writers are Alan Garner, who uses Celtic myth in *The Weirdstone of Brisingamen* with its sequels and *The Owl Service;* Susan Cooper, whose *Dark is Rising* series are based on Welsh Arthurian mythology. Both these writers have achieved a system of sliding back and forth, throughout the story, between reality and myth, which is admirable, as it keeps the reader linked to present-day existence (thus heightening credulity in the magic scenes) and prevents the feeling of dreamlike exhaustion and surfeit which can result from an over-rich dose of fantasy with no alleviation of common sense. (Tolkien is not wholly free from the latter fault; some readers, even fantasy enthusiasts, find the Ring trilogy hard to swallow in one gulp.)

Another myth-user is Lloyd Alexander, whose Prydain books capably employ Welsh and Breton Celtic themes.

If you wish to write myth-based fantasies, there is an enormous wealth of material to choose from: Teutonic, Scandinavian, Icelandic, Eskimo, Baltic, Babylonian, Japanese, Hindu, American Indian, Persian, are some of the as yet not-too-explored mythologies, beyond the better known classic Greek and Roman and Egyptian canons. Of course you have an advantage if you first came to your legends as a child and are deeply familiar with them; if not, you will need to immerse yourself in them *thoroughly:* read as deeply and widely as you can, finding as many different versions of the same story as possible, acclimatising yourself, until you feel free to play with them and manipulate them in your own way.

Little Red Ridinghood was my first love. I felt that if I could have married Little Red Ridinghood I should have known perfect bliss.

Charles Dickens

My second form of fantasy is the short stories (they are usually short rather than full length books) based on traditional folk tales rather than the grander mythologies involving gods, demons, and heroes.

We are all, to some degree, brought up on folk tales and have the patterns in our minds of the Three Bears, Cinderella, Beauty and the Beast, and such favourites. This kind of folk tale adapts excellently to contemporary usage and can give a lot of pleasure.

Consider the possibilities of the following: The old man who sends out his three sons into the world, each of them instructed to learn one thing. The mother who goes to market, exhorting her head-in-the-clouds daughter not to let the pot boil over (or the cakes burn). The man who owns a wonderful cat, which has the power of telling whether sick people will get well or not. The farmer so enraged by the hooting of an owl that he takes his gun to shoot it and . . . The man who hears a bluebottle buzzing inside his bed, so takes a can of flyspray or an axe . . . The three sisters discussing a young man who passes by: 'If I married him I'd give him a micro-wave grill.' 'If I married him I'd give him a 3-D TV.' 'If *I* married him, I'd give him a . . .'

The possibilities of such stories are endless, and the enjoyment is greater because humour can be brought into play.

Even in a shabby setting, there is always the possibility of heroic action.
Nicholas Tucker, *How Children Respond to Fiction: Children's Literature in Education*

A third kind of fantasy is that which is wholly invented by the writer.

This is obviously the most imaginative kind of the three named so far, because the author must construct his own world completely, starting from scratch.

So how do you set about constructing a world?

Constructing a world — or a universe — is mostly done for pleasure, and if such is your habit you probably won't need any advice. A home-made universe tends to be either a Utopia, where everything is good and perfect . . .

> There, the gumdrops grow like cherries
> And taffy's thick as peas
> Caramels you pick like berries
> When and where and how you please
> Big red sugarplums are clinging
> to the cliffs beside that sea
> Where the Dinkey-Bird is singing
> In the amfalula tree.
>
> Eugene Field, *The Dinkey Bird* from *Poems of Childhood*

or, conversely, it is as grim as you can possibly make it, so that your hero has to battle against atrocious circumstances.

Of course when constructing a universe, you do not *really* start from scratch. The imagination must make use of some basic material, however much this is disguised. But, in the work of really skilful fantasists, one is often awe-stricken at the imaginative use to which they have put their material. Kafka and Hermann Hesse lie outside the scope of this guide, but they have influenced many children's writers. And children do read Mervyn Peake, whose gothic Gormenghast trilogy is a truly remarkable work of invention (and has also influenced many subsequent writers).

The best of all possible worlds . . .

Voltaire, *Candide*

Ideas for a fantastic world? The social organisations of insects — ants, bees, spiders — or that of birds, might produce a framework. Or animals, viewed from an animistic standpoint: the life and gang warfare of cats in a modern city, rats in a sewer. Or, indeed, people from an animistic standpoint — how about a nightmare world of school, of fox-hunting, of football? One of the oddest and most original fantasies I know is Stella Gibbons's short masterpiece, *Ticky,* all set in a kind of mad Victorian regiment, a cross between Thackeray and Ouida.

Perhaps it might be possible to write a music-based fantasy? Or an undersea one?

Another extraordinary work, which all fantasy-prone writers are urged to read, is the nineteenth-century *Flatland,* by Edwin A. Abbott (now fortunately available in Dover paperback) a fantasy entirely based on the concept that two-dimensional beings will not be able to embrace the concept of three dimensions; as we three-dimensional beings find it hard to grasp the possibility of a fourth dimension.

Walter de la Mare's fantastic novel *The Three Mulla-Mulgars* (now reprinted and available in Puffin books as *The Three Royal Monkeys*) is another wholly original conception, a strange frozen world of forest through which the three heroes must travel to a kind of lost Eden, the Valleys of Assasimmon, where their father has gone. Where did de la Mare find the idea for this mysterious region? It seems to lie somewhere between Arabia and Asia, with touches of both. However he evolved it, it is a perfect example of a writer in complete command of his material, absolutely confident of every detail.

Whatever your invented world, large like that of Tolkien, small like that of Mary Norton in *The Borrowers'* world, you must really *throw* yourself into its construction, immerse yourself in its atmosphere and topography.

If magic or the supernatural are used in your fantasy (this is not essential, by the way) — if magic is used, be sparing with it.

> It came like magic in a pint bottle. It was not ecstasy, but it was comfort.
>
> Charles Dickens, *Little Dorrit*

Too many magical rules, and being obliged to remember their ins and outs, can become a terrible bore. It is like playing games with small children — 'No, no, you aren't allowed to step outside the *circle*! If you do, you'll be turned into a *shark*!!'

Rules of magic there have to be, otherwise chaos ensues, which is equally boring, but the rules must not be obtrusive, so for heaven's sake keep them simple and at a minimum.

In my opinion, a full-length fantasy novel made out of pure invention is the very hardest kind of children's book to write successfully. Approach it, therefore, with care. Richard Adams did it, in *Watership Down,* Ursula le Guin has done it in her Earthsea books; it can be done, but it is a considerable challenge.

It is generally accepted that there need not be too much emphasis on character in fantasy. As in myth and heroic legend, the main character is a hero, and his opponents are villains — fantasy tends to be straight-forwardly about right and wrong in sharp and unrelieved black and white. Children naturally enjoy this, and teenagers appear to also; perhaps they find it a refreshing change from the fine shades and unresolved perplexities of the teenage novel.

The plot of a fantasy is generally a Quest, or a series of ordeals which the hero has to undergo; and it nearly always has to do with the rectifying of some wrong.

There is a fourth category which I will call semi-fantasy, in which there is no magic or supernatural element, but the whole narrative takes place at one remove from reality because of some arbitrary set of circumstances decided by the writer. Kingsley Amis uses such a scheme in his novel *The Alteration,* imagining an England in which the Reformation never took place. Peter Dickinson does it in his Changes series, in which the whole English nation develops a paranoid hatred of machinery (there is in fact a magical cause and cure for this state of affairs, but several of the books hardly touch on that). I would also include my own Wolves of Willoughby Chase series in this category, because they take place in the non-existent reign of King James III.

Other exercises in this mode are after-the-bomb books, such as John Wyndham's *The Chrysalids,* hypothesising a rigidly Puritanical society trying to eradicate mutants; and the same author's *The Day of the Triffids,* now familiar to most because of the TV adaptation; and Russell Hoban's remarkable *Riddley Walker.*

Time travel books may be said to fall into the category of semi-fantasy. Of late they have fallen somewhat into disrepute (a TV producer I met said, 'I'll never look at another time travel book') because of over-production. The best prototype is still E. Nesbit's *The Amulet,* where children go into the past to look for the other half of the broken Amulet which will restore their parents. Nesbit went to considerable lengths of research to acquire details for her sections on Babylon and pre-dynastic Egypt; so must you, if you attempt this genre.

> Nourishing a youth sublime,
> With the fairy tales of Science and the long result of Time.
> Tennyson, *Locksley Hall*

Beyond the borders of fantasy lies science fiction proper, which falls outside the scope of this manual. These days, science fiction is highly specialised, expert, often written by scientists themselves in their lighter moments. It is an extremely profitable medium, particularly in the USA where it occupies enormous space in bookshops. If you can write it steadily, you are on to a useful income. But in order to do so you need a basic grounding in science; and scifi is not a once-off operation; you need to produce a regular body of work in order to become established.

Ghost Stories

> I wants to make your flesh creep.
>
> Charles Dickens, *Pickwick Papers*

Ghost stories (which need not be about ghosts, as fairy stories need not be about fairies) are my fifth category. They enjoy a considerable vogue at present, along with horror stories. There are a number of ghost anthologies, some of which come out regularly, such as the Barrie & Jenkins Ghost Books. If you can write a good spine-freezer, you run a good chance of having it accepted.

The trick with a ghost story is to begin at the end, with some horrific situation, and work backwards, setting up the train of events which led to the climax. There need not be too much explanation.

Remember M. R. James's *Oh Whistle and I'll Come To You* — probably one of the most frightening ghost stories ever written: the dream of the white hopping creature pursuing the man along the beach, and the bedclothes that rise up and form themselves into a fearsome shape. M. R. James never troubled to give much explanation as to *why* the ancient whistle dug out of the sand should produce this result, or, for that matter, what the animated bedclothes could have done to their victim; and it is because the whole affair is thus left unexplained that it *is* so terrifying. M. R. James is an excellent model to follow because he is entirely straightforward. He begins each story in the most prosaic, matter-of-fact way, so that the reader is lulled into cosy security and the fright, when it comes, is therefore all the more shocking.

Ghost stories, analysed, are generally to do with our senses. If your senses betray you, or seem to, you at once, on some primitive level, begin to fear a supernatural cause. So, when writing a ghost story, make use of this factor — think of something involving the five senses.

You open a cupboard door — but find yourself looking straight into space.

You hear, close to your ear, the voice of somebody long dead, reminding you of an unkind thing you once said, which you had long forgotten.

Everything that you eat begins to taste of cucumber. Why?

You step into your bath and an invisible (imaginary?) snake twines round you. Why?

You smell a scent that should be sweet and nostalgic — lavender, say — but it has the power to make you sick with terror. Why?

Ghost stories must induce a suspension of disbelief in the reader; which means that you, the writer, must suspend your own disbelief, must contrive to get yourself into the kind of atavistic fright which sometimes assails us all when we see a black shape outside the window that ought not to be there, or when the phone rings and there is nobody on the line.

Ghost stories — and fantasy of all kinds — are closely connected with dreams, so make use of your dreams freely in their construction. Dreams are a glimpse of the buried layer of us that still feels all these primitive terrors, therefore they give us a chance to provide a genuine piece of supernatural experience.

Humour

> A kiddy laughing at a joke is one of the sweetest sights under heaven.
>
> Rudyard Kipling, *Letter to E. Nesbit,* 1903

A recent survey (by British Book News) of children's order of preference when buying books for themselves reported that they bought fiction and non-fiction in equal quantities and that, among fiction, they preferred, in this order, humour, ghost stories, science fiction, fantasy, school stories, adventure, mystery, animal stories, cartoons, war, romance, poetry, and historical classics.

If you can write a funny story for children, therefore, your fortune may be made. Good ones are not often produced. Kaye Webb, for many years editor of Puffin Books, said that a good funny book for children was the rarest thing that came her way.

Bergson had a theory that we laugh when we see humans behaving like machines. Arthur Koestler said that humour consists of the collision of two different frames of reference. The most immediate example of that is Don Quixote, who, floating about in a dream of high romantic chivalry, thinks he is attacking the Moors when really he is galloping headfirst against a windmill.

But this type of humour is not always successful for children. Indeed, I can remember, as a child, being saddened, not amused, by Don Quixote, because he was making such an ass of himself, and anyway I *enjoyed* stories about knightly chivalry, and would have preferred the windmills to be Moors. So for me, the humour of Cervantes missed its mark. All I got was a feeling of letdown.

Satire, sarcasm, and irony are not appropriate forms of humour for small children. They haven't yet learned to recognise the social prejudices that are being made fun of. They take Gulliver at face value, as an adventure story.

Contusions are funny, not open wounds,
And automobiles that go
Crash into trees by the highwayside;
Industrial accidents, no.

The habit of drink is a hundred per cent
But drug addiction is nil.
A nervous breakdown will get no laughs;
Insanity surely will . . .

So the funniest thing in the world should be
A grandsire, drunk, insane,
Maimed in a motor accident,
And enduring moderate pain.
Morris Bishop, *The Anatomy of Humour*

Zany or slapstick humour is what children really relish. They are primitives. Somebody treading on a banana peel, falling in a puddle, convulses them.

The generations reared on television are also lightning-quick, far quicker than their parents, at grasping visual and verbal gags. But they may be considerably slower to follow the same kind of humour when it is written down.

The great humorists, of course, will often be engaging several different kinds of humour simultaneously.

All Thurber's characters inhabit their own separate frames of reference. So in *The Night the Bed Fell on Father,* the action involves not only the bed falling, but the reactions of the whole family, each with his or her own maniac idiosyncrasy, to this central episode. Aunt Sarah Shoaf, for instance, 'who never went to bed at night without the fear that a burglar was going to get in and blow chloroform under her door through a tube. To avert this calamity . . . she always piled her money, silverware, and other valuables in a neat stack just outside her bedroom, with a note reading "This is all I have. Please take it and do not use your chloroform, as this is all I have."' (from *My Life and Hard Times*)

Mark Twain, in *Huckleberry Finn,* devotes a good deal of space to sending up nineteenth century heroic romance, particularly the works of Scott and Dumas, on which, presumably, the young Sam Clemens was reared. Tom Sawyer is always insistent on having things done in the proper heroic manner:

> Tom said we'd *got* to; there warn't no case of a state prisoner not scrabbling his inscription to leave behind, and his coat of arms . . .
> Jim says: 'Why, Mars Tom, I hain't got no coat o' arms; I hain't got nuffin but dish-yer old shirt . . .'
> 'On the scutcheon we'll have a bend *or* in the dexter base, a saltire *murrey* in the fess, with a dog, couchant . . .'
> 'Geewhillikins,' I says, 'But what does the rest of it mean?'
> 'We ain't got time to bother about that,' he says.
>
> Mark Twain, *Huckleberry Finn*

There you have the two frames of reference: Tom's grandiloquent ideas, Huck and Jim's matter-of-factness. This, too, is combined with a lot of broad comedy in the boys' rescue of Jim, their struggles over the snakes, the rats, the grindstone, the sheet baked in a pie, and all the other appurtenances of what Tom considers a proper rescue.

Jerome K. Jerome does best at slapstick:

> I never saw two men do more with one-and-twopence worth of butter in my whole life . . . After George had got it off his slipper, they tried to put it in the kettle. It wouldn't go in, and what *was* in wouldn't come out. They did scrape it out at last, and put it down on a chair, and Harris sat on it, and it stuck to him, and they went looking for it all over the room.
>
> Jerome K. Jerome, *Three Men in a Boat*

> Name me one thing she went short of.
> Well — food. Clothes. Coal . . . Teeth.
> Frank Muir and Denis Norden, *The Glums*

Bathos — the unexpected — is a reliable ingredient of humour: Catherine Morland opening the sinister closet in Northanger Abbey and finding a laundry list; the mad duel between King Pellinore and Sir Grummore in *The Sword in the Stone* where, purblind inside their armour, they miss each other and stun themselves by each running into a tree. But in both these examples the writers are making fun of literary tradition, Jane Austen of Gothic novels, T. H. White of Arthurian romance.

> There are several kinds of stories but only one difficult kind — the humorous.
> Mark Twain, *How to Tell a Story*

A contemporary children's writer must be wary how he makes use of pastiche, because he can't be certain that contemporary children will have read the literature he is ridiculing, so half his humour will be lost on them.

On the whole, it is safer to stick to slapstick and the eccentricities of character. William Mayne is skilled at using the latter, in a poker-faced way: Rosemary, for instance, in *A Parcel of Trees,* who demarcates her space in the bedroom she shares with her sister by putting boundary marks on the carpet.

Children like funny language, or, anyway, what seems funny to them.

'We read one of your books in class once and we liked it,' some boys on Cape Cod once told me. 'What did you like in particular?' I asked. 'Where so-and-so said, "*We'll* put some ginger into his gravy,"' they said, falling about on the floor.

Kipling, whose humorous stories were greatly enjoyed fifty years ago, is subject to a different set of judgments now. His humour — nearly always concerned with revenge, somebody getting their own back, schoolboys outwitting masters, tyrants being disgraced and humiliated — strikes us as primitive, if not downright sadistic. Very different from *Stalky & Co* are Jan Mark's contemporary school stories, for instance *Hairs in the Palm of the Hand,* which is about a boy trying to work out how much time is wasted during a school day; it is inventive, detailed, closely observed, and very funny. Roald Dahl, in *Charlie and the Chocolate Factory* and *George's Marvellous Medicine,* writes exuberant wild stories loved by younger children.

It is not easy to lay down rules for humour. Either you have it or you don't.

There's a story of a World War I Punch cartoon showing two Tommies surveying a crater. 'What made that hole?' asks the newcomer, and the old hand replies laconically, 'Mice.' This example of British humour was said to have been circulated in the German trenches with the explanatory note, 'It was not mice, but a shell.'

'Gott mit uns,' chalked the Germans on their parapets, and the British replied, 'We got mittens too.'

Humour is like the wind, which bloweth where it listeth, and if you do not have your own idea for a children's funny book, I do not believe I can help you find one, beyond providing these few definitions.

Historical Novels

As readers will have observed, historical classics came bottom in the list of children's fictional preferences. The same is not quite true of historical novels by contemporary writers, but, alas, it is true that historical stories don't sell well, and unless you are a dedicated historian and dying to depict your favourite period for children, you are advised to think carefully before venturing into this field.

Which is not to say that there are not some first class practitioners now writing historical fiction for the young, and making a living. Rosemary Sutcliff writes distinguished novels about the Roman occupation of Britain. Katherine Peyton deals with the end of the Edwardian age and World War I. (Her books are also models of the teenage novel, but were not mentioned in that section because they also contain a great deal of action and are not merely studies of adolescents undergoing emotional crises.) Barbara Willard, in her Mantlemass novels, has followed the fortunes of a Sussex family through seven or eight periods of history. Geoffrey Trease has written over sixty historical novels for the young, meticulously researched and full of action.

The standard of historical fiction is now, in fact, extremely high. Gone and forgotten, thank heaven, are all those swashbuckling, shallow extravaganzas of the twenties and thirties, full of tushery and quothas and short on accuracy.

The first principle, therefore, if you are going to write a historical novel, is that your research *must* be thorough; so thorough that, when you start to write, you can put all your notes on one side and proceed without them. Nothing makes a novel drag so as the kind of detail shoved in by the author just to show he knows it. True, it is very hard — when you have discovered some interesting fact about how horn spoons were washed or arbalests were fired — not to make use of it, but unless you can introduce it without slowing up the action, then, in a children's book, it is out of place.

Chapter Nine

Moral Message, yes or no?

> How many hundred times have I denounced 'a moral purpose' in fiction!
> Andrew Lang, *At the Sign of the Ship*
> Of course I can't go about and cram a sermon into a tale, but I try to get at the same point obliquely.
> Rudyard Kipling, *Letter to a 16-year-old boy,* 1895

Whose advice are you to follow, that of Andrew Lang or that of Rudyard Kipling? Do you put a moral message into your book or not?

'We have studied your book,' a boy wrote to me once from a school in America. 'Does it have a theme, or is it meant to be read for pleasure?'

> Little girls are not so easy to fool as they used to be.
> James Thurber, *Fables for Our Time*

Personally I believe that an overt moral message is to be avoided like the plague, whether you are addressing toddlers, twelve-year-olds. or adolescents. None of them will thank you for usurping the functions of parent or teacher, whose job it is to inculcate moral and social responsibilities. A book *is* supposed to be for pleasure, isn't it? Who are you, anyway, to preach morals to the young?

> I like a story with a bad moral.
> Thomas Hardy, *Under the Greenwood Tree*

However a story is a criticism of life, as Yeats said. Your book, willy nilly, can't help reflecting your attitude to the situations and problems that you are depicting. And certainly, in a book for medium age children and under, vice ought to be seen to be punished, and virtue rewarded — or, at least, survive.

So many volumes now issue from the press low in tone and lax in morality that it is especially incumbent on all who would avoid the taint of such hurtful matter to select carefully the books they would themselves read, or introduce to their households. In view of this design, no author whose name is not a guarantee of the real worth and purity of his or her work, or whose book has not been subjected to a rigid examination, is admitted into 'The Lily Series'.

Advertisement for Ward, Lock & Co, 1880

Taboos

> Would it bring a blush to the cheek of the young person?
> Charles Dickens, *Our Mutual Friend*

What should be left out of children's books?

Very little these days *does* bring a blush to the cheek of the young person, but there are other detrimentals.

Propaganda, for one thing: concealed advertising. Quite apart from the hypocrisy of trying to plug something, either a commodity or an idea, in a work ostensibly intended to entertain children, a text containing concealed promotion is almost certain to be boring.

How about Sex?

I would not put explicit sex into books for the medium age group. (For a discussion of teenage fictional mores, see that section.) Children under, say, thirteen, are not much interested in sex, or in emotion, and all the introspection and hugger-mugger it leads to; what they want is action and character.

In the USA, over the past few years, there has been a tremendous vogue for children's books dealing with such subjects as masturbation, wet dreams, growth of breasts, onset of menstruation; one is prompted to wonder whether children's reactions aren't on a par with the comment: 'This book tells me more than I want to know about whales.' But these books certainly enjoy huge sales, so perhaps children find them helpful. However, as I mentioned in the teenage section, a climate of censorship and restriction is now creeping back.

Judy Blume, who has written a number of informative books of the kind mentioned above, said in an interview that she was shocked to encounter a seventeen-year-old girl who knew nothing about masturbation: 'that a girl of that age should know so little about her own body' (*The Pied Pipers*). Many will agree with Judy Blume that, for their own protection, the young should know all there is to know. Others may think that the seventeen-year-old girl was perhaps better occupied passing her exams. Everybody has to make their own judgment in these matters.

Tragedy in a children's book?

Perhaps. Children have tough moral fibre. They can surmount sadness and misfortune in fiction, especially if it is on a grand, heroic scale. And a fictional treatment may help inoculate them against the real thing. But let it not be *total* tragedy. Your ending must show some hope for the future.

At all costs avoid accidie, depression, despair. These should never be allowed to find their way into a children's book. Depression is much more complicated and damaging than fear or grief, because harder to resolve.

Violence? No. Certainly not in a contemporary setting. Violence may enter at a long-distance remove, in a historical or fantastic context. But *never* present-day violence in a familiar setting. Violence is too easy to imitate. No responsible children's writer would wish to feel that he or she might have put the idea for a crime into a child's mind. 'Saw it on telly' is all too common: 'Read it in a book' would be even worse.

Final Advice

> I am screaming out loud all the time I write and so is my brother which takes off my attention rather and I hope will excuse mistakes.
>
> Charles Dickens, *Nicholas Nickleby*

Last precept. Never put in anything that bores you, for you may be sure it will bore the reader. *Love* what you write. The reason why I put in the above quotation is that you can see Dickens wrote it with extreme pleasure. You can feel his smile as the idea came to him and he put it down. You can feel this smile in plenty of other children's masterpieces — in Jemima Puddleduck, and James Reeves' poem *Cows* and Jane Austen's youthful history of the kings and queens of England and Helen Cresswell's *The Nightwatchmen,* to pick a few random examples. And there's a serious counterpart to the smile — a kind of intensity — you feel the author's awareness that he is putting down *exactly* what he intended — for instance in Ruskin's *The King of the Golden River,* and *The Mouse and His Child,* by Russell Hoban, and *Life with Lisa,* by Sybil Burr.

Really good writing for children should come out with the force of Niagara. It ought to be concentrated; it needs to have everything that is in adult writing, but squeezed into smaller compass, in a form adapted to children's capacities, and at shorter length.

But the emotional range ought to be no less; children's emotions are as powerful as those of adults, and more compressed, since children have fewer means of expressing themselves, and no capacity for self-analysis.

A children's story ought to put life in perspective. It is the first step towards abstract thought.

Children read their books over and over, very slowly or very fast; they gulp books or chew them, they believe passionately in the characters, and participate. In order to stand up to all this wear and tear, a book need almost be tested in a wind-tunnel before being handed to them. Furthermore, if it is going to be read and re-read over a span of perhaps ten years, a book needs to have something new to offer at each re-reading. A lot of children will miss humour in a story at first reading while they are concentrating on the plot. Richness of language, symbolism, character — all these may be noticed for the first time and appreciated only at later readings. Conversely, anything poor or meretricious or slipshod may be missed while attention is held by the excitement of the story, but will stand out hideously on a later reading.

Reading aloud, of course, is the ultimate test, so try your work in this way. Read it, not to a single child, but to a group of five or six, if you can get hold of them. Discover what bores them, what holds them.

Sit in the public library and watch children in the process of taking out books. Lurk in the children's section of bookshops watching customers. Go to your local school or youth club and ask if you can talk to the age group you are interested in, find out about the books they like. (You may have some surprises.)

Decide whether you would rather be set to entertain a group of adults, or the same number of obstreperous ten-year-olds. If the latter, you are probably a children's writer.

In which case, almost everything I have been saying is probably well known to you. And if not, nothing I have said is likely to make you begin.